A Spiritual Renewal

A Journey to Medjugorje

A Spiritual Renewal

A Journey to Medjugorje

Alberta H. Sequeira

Riverhaven Books

www.RiverhavenBooks.com

A Spiritual Renewal is a reprint of *A Healing Heart: A Spiritual Renewal* (2006) ISBN#1-4241-4458-2

Cover photograph: Apparition Hill
by Alberta Sequeira, Medjugorje, 1998

Published in the United States by Riverhaven Books,

www.RiverhavenBooks.com

ISBN: 978-1-937588-05-2

Printed in the United States of America

by Country Press, Lakeville, Massachusetts

Edited by Deb Kurilecz, Riverhaven Books
Designed by Stephanie Lynn Blackman
Whitman, MA

Reviews, praise for
A Healing Heart: A Spiritual Renewal

~ Cheryl Ellis, Allbook Reviews
*A Healing Heart s*hows us that there are many excuses in life that we use to leave our faith behind or question God's very existence; disillusionment with our political and religious leaders, personal tragedies we cannot comprehend, war itself, let alone the horrendous war crimes committed against our fellow man. *A Healing Heart* will enlighten many families about the benefits provided by accepting help from the Hospice Association. I would highly recommend this book to readers of all faith and spiritual viewpoints.

~ Steven Manchester, Author, *The Unexpected Storm, Jacob Evans, Pressed Pennies, Bella Bean*
I was very impressed with Alberta Sequeira's memoir *A Healing Heart.* The writing is honest and familiar, while the story is easily relatable and quite real. As a once converted Catholic who is now repulsed by the Church's recent scandals, I appreciate the message of awareness and found her faith refreshing. From the depths of a daughter's love to the nail-biting journey to Europe, it is a tale of love, courage and unyielding faith. I am sure her father would be very proud!

~ Bambi Andrade, Reader
At a time when obscenities are accepted and the mention of God, to some, is offensive, I had the pleasure of reading this fascinating book about faith and spirituality. It's a wonderful book about a woman's journey back to practicing her religion, while reflecting on her father's life as well as her own, at the time of his passing. The author tells the heartfelt story with tremendous emotion and the trip to Medjugorje will have you unable to put the book down. I am looking forward to her next book.

In memory of my father,
Brigadier General Albert L. Gramm, Sr.

Dedication

This book is dedicated to my beloved father, who had more of himself to be explored than I realized. I'm grateful for his teachings of the importance of family, faith in God, and his guidance in my growing years.

To my beloved mother, Sophie Gramm (deceased);

To my siblings and those who they have made a part of our family through marriage: Bob and Leona Waltman, Walter Gramm (deceased), Albert Gramm, Maria Gramm, Bill and Sharon Gramm, and Joe and Marge Gramm;

To for the grandchildren and great-grandchildren of Al and Sophie : David, Danny, Debbie, Lori (deceased), Brandon, Olivia, Molly, Joseph, Meagan, Michael, and Kerri;

To my wonderful husband, Al, who has leant me strength and given me love.

Acknowledgements

I will place my law within them, and write it upon their hearts; I will be their God, and they shall be my people.
Jeremiah 31:33

A *Spiritual Renewal* contains my thoughts and beliefs and is, I hope, a witness to the actions of God in our lives. This journey wouldn't have happened if I hadn't responded to Him. It was through the silence that I had opened my heart to listen.

I am indebted to all who supported me through my years working on this book. First, I want to thank my family who understood my desire to leave the military background of my father to our grandchildren and future generations of the Gramm family.

I give my deepest love to my husband, Al, who lifted me when I lost confidence and gave me the strength to go on.

I'm forever grateful to my brother, Joe, for all his hard work and devoted attention in editing the pictures and for his help in retrieving the military information on our father.

I'm thankful for my dearest friends, Arlene Albert of Vero Beach, Florida, and Eddie Sousa of West Warwick, Rhode Island, for their years of encouragement and faith for me to get my book into print.

A sincere thank you goes to my editor, Deb Kurilecz, for her talent in my final editing.

A heartfelt appreciation goes to my writer's group from Baker Books in Dartmouth, Massachusetts, for their critiques which aided me immeasurably in writing this book.

A sincere admiration to the comrades of the 26th Yankee Division who fought alongside my father during WWII, and to those who aided in contributing to this book: Joe Devine, James C. Haahr, Author of *The Command is Forward: the 101st Infantry in Lorraine*, Retired Lieutenant Colonel Fred N. Kawa, Dennis J. O'Brien, Bernard Huntley, Richard I. Paul, and Jim Neville, Curator of Camp Drum, New York

Introduction

As a child, I prayed with confidence and faith; nothing was impossible for God. As the years passed and I got older, I looked at life differently with its hardships and disappointments. Life became a reality with sadness from losing a parent, friends, and surviving a shattered marriage. My confidence turned to doubt and my faith weakened. I wondered where God was when my prayers went unanswered.

I had to remind myself that no matter how hard things were, God always answers our prayers. It will be in His time, will, and way. Birth, life and death are stages we travel through until we return once again, to our Maker.

We must never give up praying, for if we do, we'll not return to our faith or receive the many gifts and graces that await us. We must pray, not only to survive, but so we can unite and come closer to God.

—Alberta H. Sequeira

Brigadier General Al Gramm
March 27, 1910 – October 19, 1990

Dear Lord,
There's a young man far from home, called to serve his nation in time of war, sent to defend our freedom on some distant foreign shore. We pray You keep him safe, we pray You keep him strong, we pray You send him safely home... for he's been away so long.

http://www.faithfulcross.com/soldiersprayer.html

Contents

Coming into Medjugorje

And then it came into view...M*edjugorje.* The chartered bus with thirty-five enthusiastic pilgrims moved slowly down the narrow dirt road. Multiple private stone homes bordered one another on the side streets. Contrary to what I expected, the village was silent and peaceful. I thought the area would be noisy with crowds of pilgrims.

From the right side of the bus, Cross Mountain, often called Krizevac, (which means Mount of the Cross) faced me. This wasn't any ordinary mountain. The huge, sixteen ton concrete cross on its ridge was the famous landmark where so many miracles were said to have happened.

Cross Mountain tower is 520 meter-high above Medjugorje. On March 15, 1934 local parishioners constructed the cross 8.56 m (nearly 30 feet) high. On the cross is written: To Jesus Christ, Redeemer of the Human Race, as a sign of their faith, love and hope, in remembrance of the 1900 years since the death of Jesus.

That location was supposed to be the highlight of my pilgrimage, along with a climb to the top before my trip was over. The peak seemed so far off, yet, the plateau stood out so magnificently.

It was May 1998 and I tried to grasp the reality of being here. Months ago, I never would have imagined that my own miracles would bring me to this tiny, remote village in Bosnia. I didn't suspect that my life would be changed forever after my experience witnessing the visionaries having apparitions with Our Blessed Mother Mary, Queen of Peace.

I first learned about Medjugorje in 1988 during a summer cookout when my twin brother, Albert, brought a video to my parents' home in East Falmouth, Massachusetts. The video showed six young children; Ivan, Jakov, Marija, Mirjana, Vicka, and Ivanka, ages ten to sixteen years old who were having daily apparitions with Our Blessed Mother since June 24,1981.

Our Lady has given four of the six visionaries a total of ten secrets (as of 2011) about events that will happen on earth in the near future. There are two visionaries that have one more secret to receive. Some of the privileged information pertained to the whole world while some concerned the visionaries themselves or the local village. The visionaries have not revealed if they are all receiving the same ten secrets.

Our Lady has given permission for the visionaries to share only the third and seventh secret with the world. The third secret is when Our Lady promised to leave a supernatural, indestructible, and visible sign at the place of Our Lady's first apparition in Medjugorje on the hill Podbrdo at the conclusion of the apparitions. The seventh secret disclosed that an evil faced the world but was eliminated due to prayer and fasting. And lastly, the visionaries said that the ninth and tenth secrets are chastisements for the sins of the world. They can't be eliminated as the seventh secret was but can be lessened by our prayers and fasting.

She still appears to them every day, wherever they are, at 5:40 p.m. during daylight savings time, and 6:40 p.m. the rest of the year. Once a visionary receives all ten secrets, Our Lady appears to them once a year for the rest of their lives.

Ivanka received her tenth secret in May 1985, and her anniversary date is on June 25th each year. And for Mirjana who received her tenth secret on Christmas 1982, Our Lady appears to her each year on March 18th. Our Lady has also been appearing to Mirjana on the 2nd of each month since August 1987 for the purpose of praying for all unbelievers. Mirjana tells us that it's very important that all of us pray for the world's unbelievers, who are described as those who have not yet experienced God's love.

My family sat and watched the tape that Albert had brought to my parents and learned that Our Lady was telling us, "Dear children! I call you to decide completely for God. I beseech you, dear children, to surrender yourselves completely and you shall be able to live everything I am telling you. It shall not be difficult for you to surrender yourselves completely to God. Thank you for having responded to my call."

In February of 1988, Our Lady told the visionaries, "Dear children! Today, again, I am calling you to prayer to complete surrender to God. You know that I love you and am coming here out of love so I could show you the path to peace and salvation for your souls. I want you to obey me and not permit Satan to seduce you. Dear children, Satan is very strong and, therefore, I ask you to dedicate your prayers to me so that those who are under his influence can be saved. Give witness by your life. Sacrifice your lives for the salvation of the world. I am with you, and I am grateful to you, but in heaven you shall receive the Father's reward which He has promised to you. Therefore, dear children, do not be afraid. If you pray, Satan cannot injure you even a little bit because you are God's children and He is watching over you. Pray and let the rosary always be in your hand as a sign to Satan that you belong to me. Thank you for having responded to my call."

My father and sister, Leona, stayed in the living room and discussed with me the wonder of this supernatural incident happening in Bosnia while the others, with no reaction got up and went outside to relax. Leona and I had the desire to go to Bosnia but feared flying. I thought it would be a blessing if I could go to Medjugorje and be in the visionaries' presence at the very moment Our Lady was appearing to them. The possibility of traveling so far away seemed out of my reach back then.

Now, the trip was real, and my feet were about to step onto holy ground. I became blind to the other passengers who were already standing up to be the first ones off the bus as it slowed coming to our destination. My eyes searched out my window for the famous St. James Church and Cross Mountain that I had viewed a hundred times in my video. To my right, the church steeple stood above the tall trees and people walked in that direction. Suddenly, a spiritual feeling being in Medjugorje overwhelmed me. Tears of happiness started to surface.

The coach pulled up to the side of the dirt road that had no sidewalks. There were multiple two and three-story homes close together. We pulled in front of a white stone three-story home. A group of tall Maple trees were on each side of the walkway to the house. This is where the group of pilgrims on my tour would be staying for the full ten days. We were told by our tour guide, Charlie Toye from the Spirit of Medjugorje Tours of Reading, Massachusetts, that the house was owned by our hosts Nada and her son Neven Cililc.

The owners in the village opened their homes to pilgrims because Our Lady asked them to welcome the multitude of people who would be arriving at Medjugorje. Our hosts offered to wash clothes as long as they were left outside our door. Each day, a full breakfast and dinner were prepared for us.

Once the bus came to a stop, I could see across the street where a thick crowd of pilgrims was walking from every direction toward St. James Church. I had never witnessed so many people going to worship. Parents carried young children. Priests led large groups of teenagers. The sick were pushed in wheelchairs, the crippled carried on stretchers, and priests kneeled on the stone pavement with their hands over people, blessing them. To the left of the church were hundreds of outside benches filled to capacity with people praying.

I studied the magnificent St. James Church the famous place was where Father Jozo had protected the six visionaries from the police. The law enforcement persecuted not only the visionaries, but their parents, relatives, the parishioners, priests, and the pilgrims who were staying in Medjugorje.

The visionaries were taken for police investigations and psychiatric examinations, but the tests always stated that they were healthy, the same conclusion made after further examinations done in the following years.

On August 17, 1981, two months after the apparitions, Father Jozo was arrested. A Communist court sentenced him to prison to three and a half years of hard labor. He endured eighteen months of horrendous torture and was released on the condition that he never returns to St. James Church as a pastor.

St. James Church was the *Heart and Soul of Medjugorje.* Our churches back home should make us feel the same as this holy one. When I was a teenager, I remember when ushers were needed to help people find seats in church because so many people attended. Not today. I see many elderly, but where are our children?

The two heavy front doors of the bus opened with a loud, long swish sound as the air was being compressed from the tires, lowering the steps for the passengers. After a three hour drive from the airport in Split, people were anxious to exit the doors. The driver opened the outside compartments and stacked the suitcases on the side of the dusty lane for each owner to claim.

Charlie Toye started to call out each person's name and gave the numbers of their assigned rooms on all three floors. He was in his late seventies and a devoted Catholic with strong religious beliefs. Charlie was a thin man, completely bald with wire-rimmed glasses, dressed casually in jeans and a red and black plaid cotton shirt. Charlie had been a tour guide for seventeen years and brought hundreds of pilgrims to Medjugorje

With a fast glance around the area, Medjugorje seemed like a small village. Hopefully, the planned sites we were going to visit would be within walking distance. Only a few passing cars traveled down the empty road. Taxis were parked and lined up along the main street. I gathered they would take the visitors to other points of interest outside the area.

My daughters, Debbie and Lori, had bought me a new suitcase for Christmas to take on my trip. The travel case was the largest in the bunch and required two men to carry it up to my room on the second floor. The weight never occurred to me while packing my clothes. After the men delivered the carry-all to our door, they remarked how relieved they were that the bag didn't have to leave the room until my departure.

I shared a room with Arlene Albert from Warwick, Rhode Island. She was in her middle sixties, an attractive woman with medium-length blonde hair. She loved clothes and was very organized with coordinating outfits. Arlene had a great sense of humor and laughed at her own mistakes and had a positive outlook on life.

Our bedroom space was comfortable and contained three single beds, a bathroom, and a closet with extra blankets and towels. The bathroom shower had a cement floor, and a large, circular ring held up the curtain. We had heard that the water for the showers was limited because it was impossible for the water supply to handle the amount of people who come and stayed at the host homes.

As Arlene and I placed our belongings in our designated areas, we heard deafening laughter and conversation from our fellow pilgrims getting settled in their chambers. Loud smashes echoed as the suitcases bounced up the steps to the third floor above us.

A priest was always invited to accompany a Catholic group as their spiritual guide on trips to holy landmarks. Charlie Toye had invited Father Joe Whalen from Connecticut to accompany our excursion. Fr. Whalen had a white beard, mustache and eyebrows. He had a smile for everyone. Father was born in Quincy, Massachusetts and received his call to the priesthood late in life. On September 9, 1989, at the age of 66, he was ordained a Roman Catholic priest by Bishop Alfred Hughes and became a LaSalette Missionary. His ministries are many and he is a champion of the sick, the elderly, drug addicts, alcoholics, families, and those in need. He's the founder of the renowned Archangel St. Raphael Holy Healing Ministry. Fr. Whalen has spent his entire priesthood healing and helping people to find hope in their faith with life challenges.

Fr. Whalen settled in his bedroom next to us, and Arlene and I chuckled thinking his hopes of having a quiet trip and getting his nights' sleep would be a miracle surrounded by so many loud, talkative women.

Enthusiasm for the up-coming events had everyone talking to each other about where we were going to visit and who had been to Medjugorje before this trip. Our arrival erased our fatigue after the long flight. Resting wasn't in my thoughts.

Outside the house the main street was lined with vendors selling religious items. Individuals from all over the world were either entering or exiting S. James Church in a constant flow. If our churches or adoration chapels back home were attended like this, we would be living in a different world.

Arlene explained how the church fills to capacity in minutes. "We may not find a seat together when we go to Mass. Get into a pew as soon as you can. Don't wait for me."

Outside speakers were placed around the church so the people sitting on the benches outdoors could hear the priest give the services. Mass was celebrated every day between 7 a.m. and 11 p.m. Mass was said in seven different languages; Croatian was said at midnight, and Arlene said the people still didn't want to leave after Mass.

Arlene and I sat on a bench outside and watched the people walking around the area. A Mass was being said in Croatian and the language was beautiful, almost like music.

Next to the church was a gift shop that carried hundreds of books and gifts. Many were written by Fr. Slavko Barbaric, and I couldn't wait to hear him speak to us. I bought *Follow Me With Your Heart* by Fr. Slavko in case there was quiet time to read.

Fr. Slavko Barbaric was a trained psychotherapist, who was sent to Medjugorje in1983 to investigate the apparitions. For many years, he became a faithful believer and the spiritual director to the visionaries. He greeted the pilgrims and organized the daily liturgy with talks in many languages with inspirational rosary and Eucharistic adoration meditations. He wrote many booklets with themes derived from the apparitions, such as prayer, fasting, Eucharistic adoration, the Stations of the Cross and confession. Fr. Slavko made missionary journeys all over the world, which often was accompanied by one of the visionaries.

After we purchased our books, we walked back to St. James Church to sit on the outside benches. At least ten confessional enclosures outside the church had large lines with people waiting to disclose their sins to a priest, which Catholics call confessions. Above each door was a sign showing which language the priest spoke. The stations were tiny with just enough room for the priest to sit in a small chair with a thin, black drape to divide the person from him as they knelt on a kneeler.

A few people who stepped out from the confessional enclosures seemed to radiate serenity, holding rosary beads in their hands. Others walked out with red eyes, probably from crying after having a weight lifted from their soul and being given a new life.

Our first night at Medjugorje fell on Pentecost Sunday. As the darkness settled in, the Crucifix on Cross Mountain was all aglow like a red, hot coal. Though, witnesses who made the climb to the top said the cross did not appear to be illuminated. From miles away I saw long lines of pilgrims ascending to Cross Mountain with their flashlights on.

At the end of the evening, a few of us from the tour group congregated at Viktor's Restaurant. The diner was located four houses down from where we stayed. The only seating was outside under a straw roof. About six rows of two eight-foot tables were connected in the small, cramped area. The tightness added to the comfort of meeting other people and mingling with pilgrims from around the world. Arlene and I had ice cream sundaes nightly, and the habit continued until our last evening in Medjugorje.

Strangers talked openly to others about why they had made the trip to Medjugorje. Jeff Gallagher was one of them. Arlene and I met him while eating at Viktor's Restaurant the first night. He decided to tell us his story as the three of us walked back to our house.

Jeff was a handsome, tall, slender man in his late thirties. He kept a close-shaved, brown beard and mustache. He had had the same excitement coming to Medjugorje as each one of us when we realized that we were being called by Our Lady.

8

Just a month before his scheduled date to leave on his trip, Jeff had an accident while driving his company truck. He developed severe neck injuries and the doctors didn't know if he would ever be able to walk again.

He looked at us and said, "I'm really not supposed to be here."

Jeff described what had happened to him the previous night when he decided to climb up Cross Mountain.

"I was going up by myself with a flashlight, because I wanted to give thanks to Jesus for healing me and giving me the health to make this trip."

He offered up his sins by making the climb barefooted, enduring the discomfort and pain while he stepped on rocks that were wet, slippery, sharp or jagged. There were no clear pathways for walking to the top. The people in the village have kept the paths as nature created them. Pilgrims have descended countless times with their feet bleeding.

Jeff said, "When I was halfway up the mountain, a miracle happened."

Only joy showed on his face when he spoke. "I heard a crowd all around me yelling, cheering and condemning Jesus to be crucified. I was given the power to not only hear the rocks being thrown at Jesus, but the cursing against Him. I could hear every individual's voice. I had no doubt that God gave me the controlling force to hear the people who had actually condemned Him to His Crucifixion."

I asked Jeff if it frightened him and he remarked, "For some reason, it didn't. I just kept asking Jesus over and over again to forgive me for my sins as I continued up the mountain."

Certain people were chosen by Our Lady and Jesus to witness something beyond our world. This was Jeff's time.

He looked at us and said, "This experience will help me the rest of my life to trust in the All-Powerful and Almighty God."

We stopped in front of our house thanked Jeff for sharing his story. I could see his contentment from sharing the blessed event with us. He waved and went off in another direction. We never saw him again during our stay, but he was someone who touched my life. Like me, he was another person who had faced and combated roadblocks before his trip.

I never wanted the night to end and had no desire to sleep. If it were possible to exist without rest, I would have stayed awake completely. Nightfall became a special time for me because of the peacefulness in this village. Sounds coming from the people singing in St. James Church became embedded in my mind. Our bedroom faced the lane, and when I lay in bed, everything became so still I could hear the sound of tires from each vehicle passing slowly over the stones in the dirt road.

The evening was so quiet that when people returned late to their assigned homes, I could hear them picking up pebbles with their shoes as they walked on the dusty pavement under my window. The whispers from their private conversations echoed into our bedroom. The atmosphere gave me such a rush of tranquility that it would send me into a deep, relaxing sleep.

Medjugorje wasn't just a place of sounds. This village filled my very soul spiritually when I saw people walking with their rosaries in their hands, praying from the heart, attending Mass at St. James Church; not once or twice, but all day long, and being in the Holy Spirit sharing Adoration with Fr. Slavko.

Back home evenings were filled with rushing to do errands and fighting traffic after work. The night ended watching television and going to bed around 9:00 p.m. I never took the time to find a quiet corner to pray.

After spending less than twenty-four hours in Medjugorje, I could sense a change in myself. Spending time alone and completely separated from both my family and my routine showed me that I became closer to God being in a noiseless place with no distractions.

Arlene and I settled in our room. Our beds started to look good. It had been over 24 hours since we had a full night's sleep. But for some reason, when the lights went out, we suddenly had energy and acted like teenagers. I felt like I had at pajama parties in my younger days. Complete foolishness had us in tears from laughter. I couldn't remember the last time that my stomach ached from something comical.

I started to observe the pleasure of being with Arlene. Putting the fast-paced world behind made me see that my husband, Al, and I took everything in our lives too seriously. We didn't find humor in our mistakes or with the silly things that happened to us. I started to see that life should be taken more lightly, and how important laughter is in our lives to take away stress.

The house we stayed at in Medjugorje on the second floor

Ed Sousa and Arlene Albert   Arlene and Alberta

St. James Church

The next morning, I woke to the sounds that engulfed me going to sleep. People were already up and heading to the services at St. James Church, visiting the visionaries, or taking a stroll alone to pray. The music from the church was already being heard from the house. It was a peaceful location and not once did I hear children yelling or horns blowing from the few cars that did pass through the village. I looked to my left to see if Arlene had awakened. She was doing the same; listening to the sounds of Medjugorje.

"Good morning, Arlene. I see you're awake. How did you sleep?

"Like a log. How about you?"

"I haven't felt this much contentment in a long time. If only we could have this much time at home without rushing and putting material things first. What's our schedule for today?"

"A good breakfast, I hope, because I'm starved, and then we're scheduled to meet the visionaries' cousin, Draga Ivankovic, after the 10 a.m. services. I'm going to jump into a shower first."

"Okay. I'll pick my outfit out," I said jumping up with excitement to face our morning. "Looks like a beautiful, sunny day."

"I think it's supposed to nice the whole week."

It wasn't long after when I heard Arlene laughing.

"What's the matter?" I asked.

"This is going to be a challenge taking showers. The curtain enclosure isn't staying up."

"You're kidding!"

"We're going to have to sit on the cement base of the shower floor. I hope the water doesn't go over the bottom rim."

We joked about the dilemma instead of bothering the owners of the household. The inconvenience was offered up as a sacrifice.

Arlene and I walked downstairs to the dining area, where our tour group blended in deep conversations. I was surprised to see the room filled so early with people eating breakfast. There were no special seating arrangements, giving everyone an opportunity to mix in with different people during each sitting. This gave us a chance to get to know new people each day.

Father Whalen started each meal with a blessing over the food placed on the tables and the people preparing it. Our Lady asks us to fast each Wednesday and Friday only with bread and water, so bread was the main entrée for those who gave up a big meal during their stay. Fasting on those days was something I couldn't do, or maybe I didn't try hard enough.

Butter and jellies accompanied the assorted homemade breads. Fresh oranges, strawberries, apples and bananas filled large, decorative bowls. Sometimes hard-boiled eggs were served. I was never disappointed or had the need to search for more. Coffee, a variety of juices and water were the only drinks. Soda was never on the dining room tables but was available in vending machines outside. I found it odd for modern vending machines to be in Medjugorje but maybe there had been a request from many of the large groups of pilgrims.

Arlene and I started our morning with the 10 a.m. English Mass at St. James Church. The front entrance and the two side doors already had an eager crowd lined up, waiting. The Croatian Mass just ended. Once the doors opened, it didn't take long for new pilgrims to learn that the seats at the service were taken up within minutes.

In 1897, St. James Church, though tiny, was adequate for the village as a place of worship. From 1936-1966, construction of the church was delayed due to WWI, WWII, and Yugoslavia's civil strife. Finally, on January 19, 1969, the church was blessed even though the interiors weren't finished. The people wondered why such a large structure was necessary for this small village. The answer came after June 24, 1981 when Our Lady appeared to the six visionaries. Once the event spread around the world, and large groups of pilgrims started to come to Medjugorje, the villagers understood Our Lady's plan. Now, to their amazement, the church had become too small.

Just before the doors opened, Arlene stated, "Grab any seat available. If you hesitate for a second, every seat will be gone. We'll meet outside after Mass."

All three doors of the church opened and people tried to get in at the same time the crowd tried to exit but the crowd was controlled without anyone getting angry or being rough. I had no choice but to follow the person in front of me because people gently pushed forward from the back of the line.

I spotted Arlene on the left getting into a pew up front. We were separated and I was suddenly fighting to find an open seat. I fought fear that was trying to overtake me. Years ago, I had a panic attack in church and since then, I hated to be closed in between people. Parishioners were coming from every direction and rushed to fill any free section. It seemed the church was full in seconds, not minutes.

I had to grab a seat before they were all taken. A couple followed right behind and pushed me further in the pew. People were shoulder to shoulder leaving no room to place any belongings on the seat. Charlie had told everyone not to wear shorts or short-sleeve blouses to church, no matter how hot the temperature might be. Pilgrims were dressed with respect in God's house of worship.

I felt like a sardine and took a deep breath to control the sensation of being squeezed and imprisoned in the enclosed area. The steps at the foot of the altar, the center and side aisles were thick with a standing crowd. Worshipers swallowed up any open area in the church. Tiny canvas folding seats were positioned at the end of the pews. Pilgrims spilled out the doors and others sat on the outside benches to listen to the Mass from the speakers around the church. I never in my life saw a gathering so enthused to enter a church.

Within minutes, thirty to forty priests dressed alike in red and white garments approached the altar. Seeing so many priests from all around the world, in one location, adoring Jesus made my heart burst with love. I felt an inner devotion and an instant connection to the Holy Spirit deep within me. Every person was there for one reason; to honor our Heavenly Father. The sight of so many priests that filled the altar was so soul-moving. The beautiful adoration music started and everyone started singing. After I witnessed a united group of worshipers in this holy church, my emotions were hard to control, and I started to sob.

My eyes were glued to the altar, unlike Masses of my past when I wanted to study people to see how they dressed and acted.

Experiencing this passion made me imagine how the visionaries must feel when they actually see, hear and talk to Our Lady. No wonder the six children say there are no words on earth to describe their apparitions. I was so blessed to be called here to become a part of this holy service. It floored me that these miracles had been going on every day since 1981. For years, I had ignored this event.

Mass started and I relaxed, watching the priests on the altar. After the gospel was read, priests began telling their own life stories about how and why they wanted to be ordained. With each Mass a different priest would do the same. Each spoke openly without shame about the bad things they had done before making the change to turn back to God and serve Him.

One priest talked about how he had everything a man wanted; money from a high-paying job, two fancy cars, and frequent dates with different women. He was in the fast lane with drugs and alcohol. Yet, he couldn't understand why he felt something was missing from his life. It wasn't until a close friend got him to travel to Medjugorje that he found his missing piece. After his trip, he met with a priest from his church and started on the road heading toward God. He gave all his material things up and didn't look back.

15

Hundreds sang so loudly that the church vibrated from their voices. Holy Communion was served by priests at the altar, down each aisle, in the back of the church, and eleven priests walked outside to present the host to the people sitting on the benches.

It made me sad to think how empty our churches are at home. *Where are God's people?* How lucky we are that He doesn't judge us for our human faults. He waits through the years, lovingly and patiently, with open arms, for us to turn back to Him. Many people spend their life trying to find the right path leading to God. He forgives every sin, fault and weakness, even when we commit the same mistakes over and over again. God never gets tired and gives up on us. Forgiveness is a gift He gave us with His death.

When Mass ended, Arlene and I met in front of St. James Church. I couldn't believe that I managed to sit for over an hour and a half in prayer. I walked out feeling the Holy Spirit in the deepest part of my soul. Never before had a Mass touched me so strongly in my faith. I was being reborn spiritually and was very aware of the blessing.

I noticed a statue of Our Lady in front of the church and asked Arlene to join me in a prayer in front of it. We sat on one of the many benches that faced The Blessed Mother.

"What a beautiful statue." I remarked.

The sculpture was carved and painted all in white with Our Blessed Mother standing on a cloud. Her long veil came down Her back to the bottom of her gown. Our Lady's right hand is placed on Her heart and the left is held up. The statue was placed on a cement block with bright, pink roses growing in a circular area below her feet, surrounded by a large, black wrought iron fence.

"This is a famous sculpture," Arlene said. "It was curved to the exact image as the visionaries described Her to the artist. I read that each visionary sees Our Lady the same. They say She never touches the earth when She appears. She's shown here as a young girl in her twenties because that's how SHE looks. They have declared that it's impossible to describe Her actual beauty. Their explanation has been, 'Her beauty can't be described—it's not our kind of beauty—that's something ethereal—something heavenly—something that we'll only see in Paradise—and then only to a certain degree.' They give Her physical description as 5 feet, 5 inches, She's slender, around 132 pounds, from eighteen to twenty years old, a long, oval face, Her eyes are a wonderful clear-blue, and black hair. They even asked Our Lady how She was so beautiful and She remarked, 'Because I have love in my heart always."

We stayed and shared in a rosary.

Alberta and Arlene

St. James Church and Our Lady's Statue in Front
Copyright (c) Marcel Stoessel 1999

17

Visionary Mirjana Dragicevic

After the services, Arlene and I met our group at a small chapel in back of the St. James Church. This was where the visionaries had had their early apparitions with Our Lady. We waited for our tour guide, Draga Ivankovic, a cousin to four of the visionaries and a recognized authority on the events of Medjugorje.

Draga was an attractive, slim woman in her late twenties with long, straight, brown hair below her shoulders. She was dressed comfortably wearing sunglasses, a white, short-sleeve, cotton, V-neck jersey, black slacks, carrying a white sweater tied around her waist with a long strapped, black shoulder bag. She was outgoing and greeted each pilgrim holding their hands while she talked to them.

Draga, like the others, wanted no fame, but the publicity came anyway after the books and articles were written about the events. She didn't see the Blessed Mother, but devoted her life speaking to anyone who comes to Medjugorje. Draga repeats Our Lady's messages for millions of pilgrims each day. The visionaries continue to speak faithfully to pilgrims, because they're truly devoted to the Blessed Mother. The visionaries are as human as we are: they get sick and have bad days. But they gave up their lives to lead us to the endless happiness with Jesus and Our Lady.

Before the tour got underway, Draga explained the full sightseeing trip would be impossible for her. She was in her third month of pregnancy with her first child and couldn't exert herself by climbing or taking long walks.

The first visionary on our itinerary was Mirjana Dragicevic. The route to her home was on a pathway through a thinly wooded area, which led to an open field.

The region reminded me of when I was ten years old living in West Springfield, Massachusetts. As a youngster, I investigated trails in the woods behind our house with my siblings, Albert and Leona. Squirrels jumped from tree to tree. We heard birds as they flew out of the trees once we approached. We found clear, running streams as we pushed deeper into the forest and left our rural neighborhood behind. The same aroma of wild roses and the strong stench of fields of tall grass from the hot weather were in Medjugorje.

The memories brought me back to a time I had forgotten, the fun and pleasure of shared adventures with my brother and sister. We pulled long, thin grass out of the ground, and placed the skinny leaf between our two fingers, and blew through them. The blades made a whistle sound. The three of us carried pails to catch frogs in the streams. Each trip challenged us on who would find something amazing to bring home to show our parents. They were special memories.

Our tour group passed two elderly women laboring in the open grape fields and wearing veils and black dresses. I expected young girls or only men to be doing this strenuous work. Even working in the heat, they made the farming look like second nature.

I saw Cross Mountain in the far distance behind the miles of grape and potato fields. The mount was so tall, I couldn't see beyond it. Fields over-grown with red poppy flowers spread as far as the eye could see. They swayed in the light, warm breeze as if they were dancing to music. I was tempted, with my childish heart, to run and fall in the middle of them.

As we came through the end of the woods, the path continued between stone houses. The yards burst with enormous, brilliant red and yellow colored rose bushes. I had never seen roses so gigantic. I figured the hot climate in Medjugorje must have been the reason they looked so healthy. Roses are Our Lady's favorite flower and I'm sure the villagers are very aware of her preference with the blossoms.

19

We finally reached the home of Mirjana and joined others, pilgrims from different groups that had already congregated in front of her dwelling. Mirjana is married to Marko Soldo, whom she has known since they were children. They have two children. She meets with the pilgrims daily when they visit Medjugorje. She also has helped at the orphanage in Medjugorje since the war.

In ten minutes she came out and approached the white, wooden fence that surrounded her property. She had shoulder length blonde hair and wore black summer slacks with a light summer white blouse.

Her interpreter explained to us, in English, that Mirjana wasn't feeling well. She had the flu and was running a fever. She had the strength and love to talk to the crowd between coughs and she found the energy to give us a smile. On March 18, 1965, Mirjana Dragicevic-Soldo was born in Sarajevo. She's the second oldest of the six visionaries. On June 24, 1981, she was the second one to see the Blessed Mother appear that day. Her family lived in Sarajevo, and she spent summers with her grandmother who lived in Bijakodvici in Bosnia.

Her daily apparitions had stretched from June 24, 1981 until December 25, 1982. On this last date, Mirjana was the first seer to receive her tenth and final secret. Our Lady told her with the last apparition that for the rest of her life she would have one yearly apparition on March 18th. Starting August 2, 1987, on the 2nd day of each month, Mirjana hears Our Lady's voice. The prayer intention that Our Lady confided to her is for unbelievers…those who have not come to know the Love of God.

Mirjana spoke to the group. "So many priests have lost their way. In Medjugorje we always show respect for our priests. Never speak ill of them…pray for them. If you're not comfortable at a church, find one that you like and worship there. Our Lady has told us, 'If you have a choice between coming to see me or going to church…choose Mass. There, you receive my Son and He's truly present on the altar in the Eucharist."

Mirjana wanted us to understand the importance of being in the presence of Jesus and receiving Him. "Our Lady wants everyone to pray the rosary and it's not enough to simply pray. It's not enough to just quickly say some prayers, so that one can say they prayed and did their duty. What She wants is for us to pray from the depth of our souls and to converse with God."

Speaking in a soft voice she said, "Our Blessed Mother wants us to pray more and we should love God as our Father. We should accept the messages of prayer, fasting, conversion, and reconciliation once a month that God's sending to the world through the Blessed Mother of Jesus. If we do this, we'll not be afraid of anything no matter what the future may hold."

Draga told us that each of the six visionaries was receiving ten secrets from Our Lady. When the last visionary received all ten, the secrets will be given to Fr. Petar Ljubicic, who was the priest chosen by Mirjana to reveal the secrets. The secrets were written on a cloth that can't be destroyed even by fire. Fr. Petar won't be able to read them without the help of The Blessed Mother. Ten days before one secret event is to occur, Fr. Petar will read them privately. He will fast for seven days. Three days before the secret happens, he will announce them to the world.

The information will be read one at a time, depending on the dates. They will name the place, dates, time, even minutes where they will occur. The secrets contained major happenings that will occur in every corner of the world. That's why prayer, fasting and going to Mass are important to help one convert. Our Lady stressed that time was running out.

When Mirjana completed the talk, she bent her head down in prayer. We stood silently as she prayed for all of us. Once finished, she smiled and turned and walked back into her home.

Oasis of Peace/Apparition Hill

After Mirjana's visit, Arlene wanted to show me the Oasis of Peace Chapel that was off a dirt road away from St. James Church. The entrance had a long, winding, cement walkway bordered with white and pink roses with yellow honeysuckle. The small shrine was hidden within a thin forest of trees.

A sign outside asked for silence upon entering. When the two heavy, wooden doors were opened, the prayer area revealed how small and empty the temple was, with only two people inside kneeling. There were ten rows of pews on each side of the center aisle. The old, uneven, wooden floors creaked as we walked. The noise echoed all around us from the stillness. I walked down to the front row.

In the far left corner, at the foot of the altar, was a statue of the Crucifixion of Jesus that was built to the actual height and size of a man. Instead of a solid porcelain figure, the sculpture had hair on Jesus' head, chest and legs. Blood was upon Him everywhere, even at the bottom of His feet, to show His excruciating suffering. Deep open lacerations and bruises were embedded all over His body in detail. The crown of thorns showed the severe and bloody injuries caused by the unfathomable gashes in His forehead and scalp.

I could see and feel the reality of His agonizing torture. I fell upon my knees at this sight. Tears rolled down my face. What an impact. For the first time in my life, I visualized what Jesus did for us; sinners who kept repeating our offenses and misdeeds toward Him. We didn't take quiet time to comprehend what He must have endured.

I was reminded of in 1346, Jesus had appeared to St. Bridget of Sweden. During a famous pilgrimage which she made to Rome at the command of her Lord, He dictated to her the "Fifteen Prays of St. Bridget," in Honor of his Passion in the church of St. Paul. Jesus appeared to her and said, "I received 5,480 blows to My Body. If you wish to honor them in some way, say 15 Our Fathers and 15 Hail Marys with the following Prayers, which He taught her for a whole year. When the year is up, you will have honored each one of My wounds." In 1391, she was canonized. These Fifteen Prayers can be found at www.marypages.com/BrigittaEnglish.htm.

I realized that no human being could have ever stood such persecution for our own sins. Jesus gave up His life for us. I asked God to forgive us for what we did to His only beloved Son, Jesus Christ our Savoir. Our sins of fear, jealousy, anger, lust, greed, and hatred killed Him. The only person on Earth, who loved us unconditionally, was taken and crucified like a criminal. I couldn't turn my eyes away from His torn Body hanging on the cross. I studied every inch of the statue from head to toe, only to see a man. We forgot this. Jesus was as human as we are. What a gift we had tossed aside.

I sat wishing that this statue could be delivered to every single church, so every person could kneel adoring Him. They would be able to gaze upon Him and see the reality of who He was and what He did for us. How weak we are for having the need to see to believe. The Bible, which is the greatest book of faith, is tossed aside by many. It's the life story of Jesus told by his chosen disciples, who not only walked on this Earth with Him, but ate and slept with Him. The Church teaches that God is Infinite. "He was, is, and always will be" (Ps 90:1-2).

After leaving the chapel, our souls were so full of peace that Arlene and I walked in silence. Our next destination was straight up the road to Apparition Hill, which is also called Mount Podbrdo. This was where Our Lady first appeared to the visionaries.

Once we reached the bottom of the hill, hundreds of pilgrims were already going up in a procession following Father Slavco. Suddenly, I became aware of the climb facing

23

me. The elevation wasn't gradual in its ascent, but started straight up from the street. There were rocks and clay three-quarters of the way up before reaching a grassy knoll. Having suffered for years with fibrillation, any climbing, even stairs could bring on an attack faster than anything else. This was going to be a trial for me but I didn't want to let Arlene know the climb was going to bother me.

I was wearing tan summer slacks, sneakers and a red cotton three-quarter sleeve shirt. This light-weight clothing was already too heavy for the hot weather and going up the slope was only going to add to my body heat. It was over ninety degrees and I was already perspiring. Having my backpack over my shoulders at least left my hands free to balance myself as we started the climb.

High above the crowd I spotted the Crucifix that was being carried up Apparition Hill as hundreds of pilgrims followed behind this holy priest. As each Station of the Cross was reached, a new person would transport the cross. We merged into the gathering, saying the rosary that was already in progress. People from different countries prayed in their own languages and our voices blended together in a beautiful tone. I could feel the love for Jesus and Mary from every stranger. I was ecstatic knowing we were going up to the actual site where Our Lady first appeared to the six visionaries.

When we finally reached the brush, the path became very narrow and thick with wild rosebushes. As I walked passed them the thorns grabbed and clung onto my thin slacks. The land leveled out into a more open area when we reached the peak. Walking on a straighter level was a relief but the section was all rocks.

Hundreds of people started to kneel around the cross that had been placed where Our Blessed Mother had first appeared. The Crucifix was erected high upon a mound of rocks and placed on the highest point of the mountain. The mountaintop was raised high above the landscape below, and the sight was breathtaking. The warm breeze gave me a slight cooling effect.

The whole village of Medjugorje spread out beneath where we sat. The land was divided into sections of open fields and plowed farmland. St. James's steeple towered above the homes, making it easy to spot.

Arlene prayed on her knees at the foot of the cross. The sun hit the steel cross directly, causing it to sparkle.

Right where I'm standing, the apparitions happened. I tried to visualize the holy incident. The visionaries had stated that they had seen Our Lady standing on a cloud. My heart leapt with both excitement and the greatest feeling of love as I tried to imagine the event.

All those around us had the same call to come to this village. Our Lady blessed each person and only asked us to pray and do whatever the visionaries relayed to us. The trip was a gift for each person standing at this divine spot.

As I sat on the top of the hill looking down upon the distant village, I reflected on how I came to know about this holy place and the reason for this trip. The spiritual change in me happened when I first learned about my father's cancer. I had never taken the time to learn about this remarkable man. He wanted to come to Medjugorje hoping for a miracle from God to cure him, but he was too sick to make the journey.

I separated from the crowd and soaked up the peacefulness. I sat on the grass facing the tiny village below and leaned back against a tree. The burning sun hit me, and I thought back to my conversation with my father in his home in East Falmouth, Massachusetts. Our talk was about miracles—miracles that later lead me to Medjugorje.

Miracles Around Us

"Dad, do you believe in miracles?"

He turned, looked at me with a shocked expression on his face, "Of course I do. Don't you?"

It was a question he probably never expected a daughter in her forties to ask. With our strong Catholic upbringing, I could see he was stunned by my doubt.

"Yes, I do believe, Dad, but I wish we lived in the times when Jesus was on earth and we witnessed Him heal with our own eyes,"

He gave me a loving but disappointed look and then turned to put down the books he carried. Slowly, he placed them back into the living room bookshelves he had just polished. He had built the unit for my mother a few years back.

Once Dad completed the task, he continued to explain his feelings on the subject. "Honey, there are miracles around us each and every day. We just don't take the time to see them. People are healed from terminal diseases when doctors had given them no hope, or a person walked when they were told this would be impossible. You can witness a mystical event without ever knowing how it happened. No one stops to realize these are miracles and that they come from God. You need to look, listen and watch more closely to things around you."

We shared this unusual subject on a beautiful, hot summer day back in June of 1987 on one of my many visits to my parents' home in East Falmouth, Massachusetts.

The sun was shining directly through the large bay window in the living room and I could feel the warmth of it through me.

I took life with Dad for granted, never realizing time was disappearing and the moments left with him would soon be taken from me.

He was always in good health and very active at seventy-nine years old. Dad was not one for sitting around in front of television all day. If Mom didn't have things for him to fix, he would find projects to keep himself busy. It took him months to build a beautiful fieldstone fireplace in the backyard. He replaced all the storm windows for their low level ranch home, and took pride with keeping the yard clean of debris.

In 1956, my father, Albert L. Gramm, Sr., retired as a Brigadier General in the Army. He had fought in WWII and was one of the commanding officers of the 26th Yankee Division. He still maintained a solid physique and loved showing off his strong, firm legs in the summer when he wore shorts. Every outfit matched and he never went anywhere without wearing one of the Cape Cod hats from his collection. He tried to hide his thinning, gray hair by combing it to one side.

Dad was always a hard person for me to get close to because he rarely showed his emotions. He was a man of very few words, but he often demonstrated his feelings by giving me a warm smile along with a wink when he passed by me. One small gesture, and yet, it made me feel so loved.

I acted no differently than him when the time came to opening up about how bad things really were during my marriage and after my divorce. My problems were locked deep within me and I never asked for help or advice from my parents.

Divorced and on my own with two teenage daughters, Debbie and Lori, decisions always faced me. I didn't want to throw any turmoil my parents' way. It wasn't unusual for my four siblings to turn to our father for advice on important matters, an act that I routinely failed to do. I felt that if I was old enough to get married, I was old enough to handle my own problems.

My siblings, Albert (my twin), Bill, Joe, and a sister, Leona, ranged in age from our thirties to fifties. Though Mom often remarked, "You'll always be kids to Dad and I no matter how old you all get."

In 1944, our brother, Walter, died at seven years old from polio. At the time, Albert and I were only two years old, and Bill and Joe weren't born. Leona, a year older than Walter, was close to him and they had done everything together. She went through her own depression as a child after losing a brother so young.

We all avoided talking about our father dying someday and not being in our lives. The fear of losing him made us act like this horrible event would never happen. I would hear of friends losing parents and my heart would go out to the family left behind. I attended the funeral, shared their loss, and went right back to my daily routine.

In October of 1990, I sat in Dad's rocking chair facing my father lying in bed, dying of cancer. He needed a miracle like the one we talked about so long ago.

I thought the death of either parent would be far distant, years from now. My mother, Sophie Gramm, was born in March 1914 in Roxbury, Massachusetts. My maternal grandmother, Zofah (Easeznska) Dzengelewski, was born in Poland and still living at ninety-five. My mother's father, Walter Dzengelewski, who was deceased, was also born in Poland. In 1910, Dad was born in Worcester, Mass. His father, Leopold C M Gramm, was born in Gardner, Massachusetts and died of cancer in his late seventies.

Dad's mother, Henrietta (Walker) Gramm, developed Tuberculosis when he was two years old. She was sent to a TB hospital in Rutland, Massachusetts, but when declared incurable, she was brought home to die.

I never learned why Dad's father didn't raise him, but his grandmother took on that responsibility until she died. By then, Dad was seventeen years old. The reality of Dad's cancer was catching up with me and there was little time left to know about his life: not only as a father and a husband but as a person. I wondered, how I had allowed all my years to go by, without ever caring to learn who he was, and what he was all about. He had to have had dreams. We all did.

I prayed as I watched him fade each day from this cruel disease. I asked God to help me find a way to heal my heart from being so selfish with my own wants and needs and from not trying to build a relationship with my father. Now was the desire too late?

Henrietta and Leo Gramm

Dad's Grandmother

Dad as a young boy

Sophie and Walter Dzengelewski

29

Family Members

During my growing years in North Dighton, Massachusetts, I watched Dad leave the house for work, always remembering to kiss my mother goodbye. The same ritual was performed upon his return after a hard day. I took no time to ask him what he did in his career. I knew he joined the National Guard in 1928 and served in the Army during WWII. I didn't know the history he carried throughout his service years.

It was rare when weekends at our house weren't filled with laughter from my parents' friends. Many of the men in the group served with Dad during the war. Every few months, the couples would take turns entertaining at their own home. Their service years were the loud topics that went around the kitchen table while the couples played cards. That was the time I should have been within listening distance to hear and learn what their lives were all about when they were young. With the devastating casualties during wartime, it was a blessing from God that our father came home alive and unharmed.

A new world had opened up for me after ending my fourteen-year marriage. I felt very independent and proud to handle all my problems without asking my parents for any help. The tension in my life dropped when I was able to make decisions with my own life and my daughters. The sad part was that I still loved my ex-husband, Richie Lopes. Before his drinking got out of hand, he was a very gentle and loving person. We all had big dreams as a family.

Our secure, happy lives turned to confusion, fear and abuse from Richie's blackouts. I had spent four years in private counseling, Al-Anon meetings, and two months of sessions with my husband in the Alcoholic Anonymous counseling program. At the end of getting help with professionals with substance abuse, Richie felt he had no drinking problem and decided not to go to AA meetings or get any more guidance. He continued his addiction, and with no hope from his denial, in 1979, I divorced him to keep myself mentally strong to bring up the girls alone after a small breakdown.

It wasn't until Richie had been hospitalized that he had admitted to his dependency on alcohol. By then, his habit was killing him. When he changed and wanted to live and stop drinking, it was too late. On February 10, 1985, he died from cirrhosis of the liver at forty-five at the VA Hospital in Providence, Rhode Island. Debbie was twenty-one years old, and Lori was seventeen facing life without their father.

Richard Lopes

In 1983, four years after my divorce, my father wanted to help me by giving me a down payment for a used car. I was determined to do everything on my own, but I swallowed my pride and decided to take his offer. He started to car hunt in the East Falmouth area, and I did the same in my surrounding locations.

This was how I met my future husband, Al Sequeira. He was a manager of a dealership I visited in Taunton, Massachusetts. As I pulled into the lot, I noticed him in my rearview mirror, walking toward me.

He wore black dress pants and a gray sports jacket with a white shirt and a silk maroon tie. Al's appearance caught my eye right away along with his masculine good looks. His black, wavy hair had a touch of gray along with his close-trimmed beard and mustache.

His taste in clothes showed his self-confidence and his smile melted my heart. Al didn't come across as being pushy with his sales pitch but was very informative and experienced in the car business. I didn't end up purchasing a car through

31

him only because my father found a Ford Escort that I loved at another dealership in Falmouth.

God works in strange ways, putting people in our paths for bigger and better things. Because of my father's offer to help me, I went out to search for a car and instead found a lasting friendship and a deep romance with Al.

I lived an hour away from my parents' home, so I wasn't available as often as I should have been to help my mother with the care of my father when he first got sick. Dad was going back and forth to the doctor's office because of discomfort under his right rib. We all thought his pain was something minor and his health was no major concern. My father thought his problem was from a gallbladder attack.

Between my siblings and I, one of us was available to help out when the need arrived. We all lived in Massachusetts and an hour was the longest it took for any of us to travel to my parents. My brother, Joe, and his wife, Marge, lived in Yarmouth, about fifteen minutes away, so they visited our parents frequently to see how they were doing. Their business, Gramm Upholstery, kept them busy but they could take time out of work whenever they got a call from my mother.

My sister, Leona and her husband, Bob, lived in Buzzard Bay and owned the Waltman Lumber Outlet in Wareham. Leona stayed in touch with Dad on a daily basis and took him to his scheduled doctor appointments.

My twin brother, Albert and his wife, Maria, lived in Stoughton and dropped by mostly on the weekends because they both had a business to run. Maria owned a hair salon, Dante's III, in Norwood, Massachusetts with her two sisters, Diane and Lisa. Albert ran his company, Gramm Sign, from their home. He made outside commercial business signs.

My brother, Bill, and his wife, Sharon, lived in Scituate and squeezed visits into their busy schedules. Bill worked for Leona at the Waltman Lumber Outlet as the company's Yard Manager. Sharon worked for a catering business that frequently serviced President John F. Kennedy's family at their compound in Hyannisport. Sharon did most of their events, and we loved listening to her talk about the famous stars that attended.

Dante and Carmela Picciano, Maria's parents, had bought a lot behind my parents' house and had built a beautiful home there. It was wonderful having the two families get together for cookouts or just everyday visits. They were also available to help.

Our parents were home most of the time and no one worried about the formality of calling first. I enjoyed the ride because of the beautiful scenery along Cape Cod, so the trip was never wasted even if they weren't home.

Family Members

Dan & David
Albert and Maria

Sharon and Bill

Joe and Marge

Bob and Leona

Mom and Dad

Debbie and Lori

Alberta and Al

Five Generations

The Beginning of the End

In 1988, Dad had surgery for cancer of the prostate at the Falmouth Hospital. After the procedure, the urologist informed him there was one percent of cancer left behind. Because this particular type of growth was very slow moving, his doctor assured him that the cancer could be controlled if the tumor came back at Dad's next physical in a year. He sent Dad home telling him not to worry.

The family begged our father to go to any hospital in Boston for a second opinion but he had complete faith in his doctor. He insisted no further tests were going to be done unless they were ordered. No amount of talking or pleading could change his mind.

We all feared Dad's condition was serious. He still kept up with chores including painting the house, mowing the lawn and any other maintenance. Dad always accomplished anything that had to be done and tackled new projects to keep active even though he had slowed down at seventy-nine years old.

Eight months after the prostate surgery my father experienced pain on his right side. Leona had had gallbladder surgery in the past and Dad spoke to her about his symptoms; thinking he might have the same problem.

After Dad informed me of his up-coming tests, I telephoned him frequently. He assured me he would call when the results came back from the doctor. In addition to his illness, we also spoke about some medical problems I was having. There was the possibility of me going into the hospital sometime in the future for surgery to remove fibroid tumors from my uterus.

Weeks went by, and I hadn't heard anything, so I called Dad. He insisted everything was fine and that he was still waiting for all the test results.

Meanwhile, the rest of the family met at Albert and Maria's house to make arrangements for a surprise birthday party for both our parents. Dad's birthday fell on March 27th and Mom's was the 28th so we always combined the celebration but this was the first really big party to commemorate their birthdays. Dad was going to be eighty years old and Mom would be seventy-six.

Joe suggested the Roadside Café in Hyannis. He had been there before and said they had a large menu and everyone could choose whatever they wanted to eat.

I invited Al to join us. We arrived at the restaurant to find a backroom had already been decorated with pink and blue balloons hanging over two long tables with flower centerpieces. Gradually the room filled with my brothers and their wives, my sister and her husband, and the grandkids David, Dan, Lori, and Debbie with her husband Brian. Maria's parents, Dante and Carmela Picciano, came to share in the event.

Dad and Mom entered the doorway with no surprised reactions on their faces; which I found odd and disappointing. I figured that someone must have tipped them off about the party. Once everyone gave them a hug and kiss, they went immediately to their seats and settled at the first table. It wasn't long before the room echoed with deafening laughter and conversations. My parents made no movement to join in the chaos.

When Leona walked toward me, I took her arm and pulled her aside asking if anything was wrong with our parents. She whispered that Dad had told her that morning that the test results showed his cancer had spread to his stomach and liver. My parents were devastated. *God, this couldn't be happening.*

What a terrible, stressful day for them to be under with a surprise birthday party. If the doctor gave good news, they would have been excited beyond words that we had done this for them. I suddenly felt sick, but kept my emotions to myself.

I didn't know who else knew and wasn't about to say anything. It would only make my parents feel worse if the news of the test results spread.

Sharon abruptly stood up and raised her wine glass. The rest of us did the same. Sharon looked directly at Dad and Mom, with the warmest and most loving smile. She said, "Happy birthday to both of you! May you enjoy and share in many, many more wonderful years together. We love you." The room filled with applause as we shouted with approval from Sharon's toast. I assumed she wasn't aware of the situation. Dad and Mom stared back with unfamiliar forced smiles on their faces.

After dinner, the waitresses brought out one large chocolate and one white cake lit with candles, and everyone joined in to sing "Happy Birthday." We all had enjoyed planning the party but our parents were probably glad when the evening ended. Their minds couldn't have been focused on the celebration. The happy and secure world they were living in just collapsed.

Dad was now fighting an aggressive stomach and liver cancer less than a year after his prostate surgery; the one his doctor told him not to worry about because the tissue mass metastasized slowly! I couldn't help being bitter and wondered if his cancer could have been cured if the doctor had done further testing right after his prostate surgery a year ago. They might have discovered that the malignancy had spread to the other organs which it obviously had done. Now he needed surgery to remove part of his stomach.

Leona went to stay at our parents' home the day before Dad's medical procedure. She and Dad shared a large bowl of grapes and after consuming half of them, he experienced agonizing stomach pain. It never occurred to them what the acid would do to the ulceration in his stomach. My sister thought he would have to be taken to the hospital before morning, but my father suffered through the throbbing discomfort until the distress subsided.

One month after their birthday party, Dad's surgery was performed at the South Shore Hospital in Weymouth, Massachusetts. Family members filled the waiting room. A nurse informed us that we would be notified of his condition when the surgery was done. In the meantime, we tried to occupy our minds by reading the magazines placed on the corner tables, but concentrating on anything but Dad was impossible, so we headed for the cafeteria to get something to eat.

A few hours later, we returned to the waiting room. When the procedure was completed, we saw Dad being wheeled from the Operating Chamber toward the Recovery Room. We all clapped and waved to him as the nurses took him down the hallway. As he was wheeled by, he gave a groggy stare in our direction.

Once he was comfortable in his cubicle, only Mom was allowed to visit him. After fifteen minutes she came down the hall toward us, smiling. She jumped straight up in the air and clapped her two feet together like a professional dancer. How she did that at her age was beyond me. Our hearts jumped with hope.

My mother informed us Dad had seventy percent of his stomach removed. She told us that when he saw her, even with strong medication, he immediately said, "Oh, Sophie, the pain is awful." The thought of him suffering was like a knife going through my heart. I left the hospital relieved knowing the nurses would do the best they could to make him comfortable.

The next day we all arrived at the hospital to take turns visiting him. When Albert and Maria entered the waiting room, I noticed Maria didn't seem like herself and had an additional aura of sadness about her, over and above our father's condition.

When Albert went in to see Dad, she suddenly whispered, "Albert went to the doctor's office yesterday and the results aren't good."

Albert had been experiencing what he thought was a bad cold leaving him with an unusually deep, scratchy voice that didn't sound normal. When he spoke, his speech was very hard to understand. It sounded like a bad case of laryngitis. My brother was in his forties and had been a very heavy smoker since he was a teenager.

His primary doctor told him he had bronchitis. Months later he strained his voice whenever he spoke and became hoarse. Albert went to another doctor at the Massachusetts General Hospital in Boston for a second opinion and the diagnosis was throat cancer.

Oh, Lord, no! The announcement almost brought me to my knees. I felt the news go right through me. Here's my twin who will be faced with a hard, painful road the day after Dad's cancer surgery. How were my parents going to handle his diagnosis?

Dad was allowed two visitors at a time for a short period. In addition to his agonizing suffering from surgery, he also fought a fibrillation problem. This was something he had dealt with since his late twenties. Doctors had been trying to find a medication to control his irregular heartbeat.

It was easy for Albert and I to understand our father's health problem. We both had had streptococcus numerous times when we were seven years old and had developed rheumatic fever from the multiple infections. Because of this, we had to have our tonsils out and were admitted into a hospital for three months. This caused us to develop heart disease and we have had episodes of fibrillation most of our lives. Both of us still take different medications for this complication.

When my turn came to visit my father, I was amazed to see how good he looked after his ordeal. He was sitting up and talking to the nurses like he was in complete charge of his arrhythmia, advising them which medications to give him from his past treatments that have made him comfortable. Through the years, he knew which ones controlled his rapid heart rate.

I sat down in the chair next to him and Albert was talking about his own cancer. They were both discussing the disease with controlled emotions. Albert explained that his doctor had offered to do an experimental radiation procedure that had never been used on anyone before. He had already signed up to be their first patient. My brother and father discussed every avenue to take with both their treatments which would be done at the same time; Albert with radiation and Dad with chemo.

I tried to chat with my father and felt uncomfortable because I was lost for words in the discussion. Albert helped the situation by staying in the room talking and my silence made me realize how little time I had spent in conversations with Dad.

Sitting there with nothing to say, made me wonder why I should be feeling this way in my father's presence. Now and then I would say something insignificant to blend into the topics going back and forth between the two of them. After my visiting time was up, I left to go home feeling empty inside.

Absent Communication

The half hour drive home gave me time to analyze why there was always a distant feeling with my father through the years. I remembered a moment when my daughters and I were leaving my parents in East Falmouth after a visit. While I hugged my father goodbye, I felt a desire to hold onto him a little longer. There was no particular reason except a sudden need to feel close after having spent a nice day with him.

My father must have felt uncomfortable because he stopped hugging me first and stepped back. I smiled and embraced him again, explaining I wanted a special squeeze. He allowed me that but he seemed stiff. Our embraces were always very fast, and I don't think he knew how to handle this unusual request.

My father's routine of saying goodbye to anyone was to go outside and stand at the end of the driveway and wave. It could have been the dead of winter and snowing, and he would never fail to put his coat and boots on to stand outdoors with his hand high in the air and with a warm smile on his face. He wouldn't go back into the house until we were out of sight. The children and grandchildren grew to know his ritual and participated in the farewell formality at each departure. They waved back until our car turned the corner.

Thinking back to this made me realize there was a soft side to Dad. Some men have no trouble expressing their feelings openly but my father hid his emotions. He supported us by helping with our personal hardships or financial problems. My mother had remarked once that our father took command of his family the way he did with the military men who served under

41

him, by making decisions. Dad wanted to help his children in any situation if he could.

I continued traveling down the dark roads to go home, and I thought back to another point in time when I was around seven years old. My father and I shared special moments when we lived in West Springfield, Massachusetts. He loved watching boxing and the program *Victory At Sea* whenever they were on television.

I would slowly edge my way over to where he was sitting. My desire wasn't to be on his lap or have a conversation with him. I longed to sit on the floor facing the television, lean my back against his chair and wrap both my arms around his lower legs. There I sat and watched the programs, with absolutely no interest in the shows, only sharing the time with him.

My father sat and smoked his pipe. How I loved the scent. He placed his hand gently on the top of my head and rubbed my hair slowly as he watched his favorite programs.

Dad smoking his pipe

Back: Mom with Alberta,
Dad with Albert
Front: Leona and Walter

Now, looking back, I realized Dad had always been there for me to develop an open relationship with him. The feeling of distance was mine by not inviting my father into my life and

42

not trying to enter his. If I had wanted to get to know him, I should have initiated private conversations with him.

I thought it was important to show him how independent I was by doing everything myself, including repairs to my own home. The doors to communication between us were shut because I never asked for help. I thought asking for assistance was sign of weakness. But what did I gain from not asking for support? There was so much my father didn't know about me.

All those visits to see my parents throughout my lifetime consisted of superficial talks.

Dad would asked, "How are you?"

"Good," I'd reply.

"How are the girls?"

"They're both busy with school and friends."

I didn't get into my problems. I never displayed openness to my parents. I should have told them the truth when I was doing awfully. Why was I afraid to admit that the bills were piling up and the girls were struggling emotionally from their parents' divorce? I started to understand that hidden problems didn't go away. How would I feel if my daughters were struggling and didn't tell me? I didn't want my wrong behavior passed down to them. The girls never saw their mother cry or show fear of being alone. I hid my feelings from them when I had been struggling to keep the family together. I never sat and talked to my daughters to grasp what they felt with their father's death. What they needed was all of us sharing our pain and needs. I wanted to keep Debbie's and Lori's lives as normal as possible. Looking back, our horrible, alcoholic family life was considered *normal.*

I started to understand my mistake of keeping our lives behind closed doors. I started to see why I had nothing to say to my father. I never once sat with him and opened up my heart about the abusive treatment I received from my husband's beatings. I suffered in silence, and so did Debbie and Lori.

Dad having cancer was probably the first thing we ever shared together. If we had been close, maybe he would have told me how he was actually doing mentally and physically with this illness. I never asked. Instead, I sat there depending completely on Albert to carry the whole conversation. I envied my brother for being so close to our father.

Facing Mortality

One Sunday afternoon, Al and I decided to make a trip to my parents. On arrival, we found the family congregated around the kitchen table talking to Mom about our father's condition. Joe, Bill and Leona had dropped by to see how Dad was doing. My father sat in an armchair in the living room alone watching television.

Al and I joined him so he wouldn't feel isolated from everyone. Entering the room, we found him hanging off his seat. I'll never forget the sight. He was on his back with his head leaning forward, causing his chin to be bent against his chest with his buttocks hanging off the seat. His elbows and waist balanced him on the bottom edge of the chair cushion, keeping him off the floor. Together we gently lifted him under his arms and placed him back into the chair in a straight-up sitting position.

He looked up at us and said in a tremendously frail voice, "I've never felt so weak in my entire life."

He had no strength to lift himself up or to call out for help.

Dad had received his chemo treatments a few weeks after his surgery. Leona told me he couldn't keep the first appointment because the thought of having the procedure frightened him so much. Our father had faced everything head on in life, except this disease. This hellish illness had weakened all his muscles leaving him helpless to get around.

I couldn't imagine what he was experiencing physically and emotionally. His suffering and fear had to be indescribable. No matter how many people were around him, he had probably felt alone.

45

Watching my father in this slow, painful progression, and not being able to do anything for him, was a nightmare that was becoming unbearable. Day after day, this incurable disease was sucking the life out of him. I started to appreciate how precious life is and what an irreplaceable gift God gives us.

Witnessing how death was attacking his body and mind, scared me into facing my own mortality, which I wasn't comfortable doing.

A few years back, I had gone through similar emotions when my girlfriend, Sandy, passed away from cancer. We were close friends until I started to slowly abandon her during her illness. This was the first time in my life someone close to me was dying.

She was in her early forties and in the last stage of cancer, losing weight rapidly. Sandy came to my house with a new pair of slacks for me to hem because she had no energy for anything. As she slipped out of her jeans, I gasped at the sight of her legs.

Sandy was a tall, thin woman to begin with, but now her legs showed only bones, and the skin on her thighs drooped downward. I became lightheaded and had to brace myself after seeing the reality of what happened physically to someone near death.

I was so frightened over losing my friend that I ran from her. Instead of being there when she needed support or someone to talk to about her depression, I'm ashamed to say, I left her facing death without me. She lived two houses around the corner and I stopped all visits. I acted on my own selfish fears. I was Sandy's age, and the terror of an early death hit me that it could happen to me. If the situation was turned around, I had no doubt that she would have been by my bedside to watch me take my last breath.

Finally, her husband called me at work. "Sandy has been rushed to the hospital by ambulance. If you want to see her, you should visit her after work. She's bad."

Before leaving work, I received a final call from a friend telling me Sandy had passed away. My nerves completely came apart, and I had to leave my cubicle to get myself back under control so I could finish my day. I started to comprehend that time waits for no one. I should have realized that her illness was about *her*, not me. Instead, I left Sandy wondering how anything could have been more important than our friendship.

We should have spent our last moments together laughing, asking for forgiveness if we hurt each other, and talking about what we had shared and enjoyed as friends. I had a chance to give and show a friend love before she died. I had been too worried about how death affected me when she was the one dying. What an awful, painful lesson I had to live with.

Now I was trying not to repeat my selfish actions during my own father's illness. He had to feel the love from his family and the security of not being left alone when he needed us the most. It's all about the dying person…not us.

Deciding Mom's Caregivers

In addition to the turmoil of Dad's sickness, Joe and Marge were trying to find a home with an in-law apartment. They wanted to take care of our parents so they could finally relax in their late years. Both of them still believed Dad was going to survive his cancer. Leona worked part-time for a real estate business and helped with the search.

Dad had already decided that they would be the best family to leave Mom with once he was gone.

Dad must have had a hard time not choosing Leona to leave Mom with because she had spent the most years tending to her. February 10, 1955, Joe was born when Bill was four years old. Mom had the boys in her middle forties with a ten year gap between me and Bill and fourteen years between me and Joe, the youngest. Leona gave up her teen years with little time for her own friends. Not once did she ever complain, even to this day.

Leona was now fifty-four years old, and the oldest. Dad worried that Leona's age was against her. My mother could live to be in her nineties like her mother. Dad thought in twenty some years, Leona's health could fade and stop her from completing the homecare that Mom would need.

Albert was forty-nine years old and his sons, David and Dan, were in their twenties and still lived at home. Albert and Maria had their businesses to run. I was next in line, also forty-nine, and my single life wasn't stable enough. At that time, Al and I had no plans for marriage. Bill was thirty-nine years old and he and Sharon were expecting their first child. The catering business Sharon worked for often called for her to

48

travel to Europe. Bill rode an hour to work and that would leave Mom alone all day. Bill and I both lacked the full time to become caregivers.

In our father's opinion, Joe and Marge were the two most reasonable choices. They had no children and Joe was the youngest, at thirty-five years old. Dad had the comfort and belief in his heart that Joe would be healthy and young enough to see Mom through her remaining years.

The perfect house was found in South Dennis, in the Cape Cod area. Because of his cancer, Dad didn't even try to bargain with the owners. He paid the asking price just to get the papers signed. My parent's home in East Falmouth was put on the market and the sale of it took a full year.

The Cape Cod home fit everything for everyone. The residence had three bedrooms, two full baths, a good sized living room and a full kitchen with sliding doors going out to a deck that wrapped around the kitchen. Above the two-car garage there was a full sized apartment with two bedrooms, one bath, living room and a kitchen where Joe and Marge would live. Their upholstery business would be run out of the double door garage. The home was a half hour further down the Cape Cod. The family now had at least an extra hour travel time and more during summer traffic.

Dad's Confession

Dad started to feel worse during his chemo treatments. Leona wanted to take him to the LaSalette Shrine in Attleboro, where priests offer Mass, healing services, and Confession. For over thirty years the Center has been a vital contributor to spiritual renewal for those seeking a deeper relationship with God.

My father hesitated, at first, to taking the trip because he said something bothered him. As time passed, he finally decided to make the drive with Leona, Mom, Joe and Marge.

When they drove into the large parking lot, Dad said in a panic, "I can't do this."

Leona replied, "You don't have to get out of the car; just sit and feel the peace."

Dad shocked everyone by admitting that he hadn't been to confession for over thirty years, even though he had been a lecturer at Mass every week and was an active and devoted Catholic. He feared death because he had fought and killed soldiers during WWII. Since the war, he thought God wouldn't forgive him and would send him to Hell to suffer.

Leona went into the main office and asked the woman if a priest could hear Dad's confession. The administrator called up to the Retreat House to see if a priest was available. Leona was told to bring him through a private entrance and not say a word to anyone where they were going. Confessions weren't scheduled yet for the day and the priest didn't want to call attention to this special request.

Dad spent twenty minutes with the priest in reconciliation, confessing his sins. When he walked out, Leona said the relief in his facial expression was plainly visible. No one asked what was said to him, but by his relaxed manner, they could see the peace of mind he had received.

He requested to travel up a path to the top of the hill behind the Stations of the Cross that were at the bottom along a walkway. The hill wasn't high but could be a struggle for him. The stations consist of fourteen crosses and stone plaques that show Jesus during each step of His Passion and suffering on the Cross. Praying and meditating in front of them shows our devotion to God.

Below the hill that my father wanted to go up is another section where at least forty stone steps lead up to a Crucifix of Jesus. Millions of pilgrims have climbed the stairs on their knees. This time, my father wouldn't be one of them. Dad was too sick and weak to climb up the steps. There was no physical strength left in his body. The family helped Dad make his private journey to God on the dirt path to the top. I know our Heavenly Father was aware of Dad's painful sacrifice and sincere piety at this time.

A Frightening Telephone Call

A month into chemo treatment, the doctor called my father.

"I'm sorry, Al, but the treatment isn't working. You need to get your things in order."

My father asked the horrifying question, "How long?"

"Two to four months."

Dad refused to believe what he heard and Mom was panic-stricken at the thought that their fifty-five years together were coming to an end.

My sister called me with the news and I felt like someone had kicked me in my stomach. I fought fear and disbelief at the same time. Since I still prayed for a miracle, my mind didn't want to absorb any of this information without hope.

I rushed to visit my parents the next night. When I entered the front door, they were sitting together on the couch in the living room watching television. Dad was holding Mom's hand. I tried to brace myself for the sight of my father. My legs felt like jelly seeing his trousers hanging off him. The pants looked two sizes too big. They were so baggy that they drooped, allowing the complete outline of bones in his thighs to show. My thoughts raced back to Sandy with the same thinness I had witnessed a few years earlier.

I couldn't believe in a few short weeks, how badly Dad's condition had worsened. I took a deep breath to compose myself before giving him a hug and kiss. Inside I was screaming with anger. I was very aware this time, however, that this wasn't about me.

Mom got up from the couch and said, "Lets go into the kitchen, and I'll make us some hot chocolate."

52

I accepted feeling that she wanted time alone with me. I followed behind her and sat at the table. She went about collecting the ingredients and the pan needed to prepare the mix. Mom's homemade hot chocolate was always delicious. Before she added the milk to the chocolate that had already been bubbling, the steam filled the surrounding rooms with a mouth-watering aroma. I took a strong whiff that instantly brought back memories.

I reminisced back to every winter when we were children and Mom would always have hot cocoa waiting for us after our return from sledding or ice skating. My siblings and I pranced into the house with all our friends. Nothing was more enticing than to see and smell the hot steaming cups of hot cocoa placed on the table. No matter how many kids there were, Mom never voiced any complaint that there wouldn't be enough to go around. After coming into the entryway wet and cold with frozen snow stuck to us, we stripped off the layers of outside clothing with incredible speed to get to the kitchen table.

Discovering marshmallows floating and melting on top of the drink, added to the treat. From the beverage being so hot, some of us would pick our cup up slowly and put a spoon into the mixture so as not to burn our tongues. The rest of us would blow on the liquid and then take short sips only to come up with a marshmallow mustache. My mother would get satisfaction from watching us enjoy her loving gesture.

I came back to reality as Mom poured my hot chocolate. I knew this time that making the treat was a big project. She wasn't wearing the same satisfied look in her eyes as when I was younger. I could see her confused state trying to do a simple thing. The months of stress and unanswered prayers had drained her.

Mom sat down at the kitchen table. Dad refused a cup, as he had done with any meal or snack that was offered to him in the last few weeks. If his taste buds had an urge for something special, Mom would immediately cook the entrée, only to see him lose his appetite completely when she served him the requested spread.

"Mom, how are you really doing?"

I had been so wrapped up with Dad that she had been pushed into the background. She had so much to deal with emotionally and physically. All of us had our partners to go home to, but my mother was trying to accept a future without her husband. I knew no matter how much she loved her children, we couldn't possibly fill his empty space.

Dad was no longer going to be there to hold her when she got lonely or comfort her when she got sick. Through the years, I had witnessed Dad sitting on the living room couch with Mom as they watched their favorite television shows and he'd rub his hand gently and slowly over Mom's neck, shoulders, or thigh without speaking a word. These were the same loving gestures he made to me when I was young. A touch is so healing and comforting, and yet taken for granted until the threat of being lost forever became a reality. Being left behind at an old age and facing life without your companion had to be terrifying.

Mom looked at me after I asked the question and didn't know how to answer me; she was lost for words.

Finally she replied, "Dad's very angry at his doctor. He refuses to believe he's dying."

"Do you want me to get in touch with Hospice? I'm sure they'll be a tremendous help to both of you."

I knew if Hospice was there for her during this hard time, they would be there to give her the added support after

Alberta, Leona, Albert, Mom
and Walter

Mom in her
younger years

54

his death. The organization could be the answer to give Mom the counseling that she had needed for years.

"Before I make a decision, I have to speak to your father. He has to approve such an important step," she said.

I watched as Mom finally started to take short sips of her hot chocolate that had sat on the table for at least ten minutes. It must have turned cold because the steam was gone. She showed no desire to finish her drink.

I worried about my mother, because Dad had done everything for her. He had offered to teach her how to drive, but she never took advantage of the opportunity. The only way she would travel outside the house after her breakdown, was if a family member was with her. Since her depression, she feared doing anything alone.

Mom never got professional help to get her confidence and independence back. I felt so bad and didn't know how to comfort her. I cleared off the table and cleaned the kitchen.

Before leaving, Mom whispered, "I'll let you know what Dad thinks of calling Hospice as soon as I speak to him."

The next night Leona called screaming uncontrollably. "I got a call from Dad, and he's all upset. Mom spoke to him about Hospice, and he snapped, 'Hospice! Why do I need them? They're for the dying, and I'm *not* dying!'"

My sister investigated the source of my father's distress and learned that I was the one who planted the Hospice seed.

Leona cried, "It took us months to convince Dad he wasn't going to die and now the family has to start giving him hope all over again because of what you did."

At the time, my concern was for my mother and I had felt all of us needed the support from this great and wonderful organization.

I finally came to accept the reality that my father was dying, but found no peace with the prognosis. I believed in miracles, but at eighty years old, God had to be calling him. No one else in the family had given up hope. Joe was already in the process of trying to find a store with natural herbs to heal him. Meanwhile, Mom was overcome with fear and walking around in a daze.

I was stunned that everyone in the family hadn't accepted the prognosis from the doctor. I seemed to be the only one facing Dad's short time left with us. He had everything against him; his age, cancer in his liver, stomach, and prostate. I felt like an enemy within the family unit for not holding onto hope.

A New Move

In 1990, legal bank papers were finally signed for the house in South Dennis, and since there were no problems, my parents wanted to move in right away on Columbus Day weekend. Boxes were now being collected by everyone so we could start packing their belongings.

For two weekends my girlfriend, Roberta Crealese, who worked with me at Perkins Paper in Taunton, helped the family get organized. She was in her early thirties with curly, red hair and blessed with a firm body from her faithful, daily gym workouts. She was energetic and enjoyed being active.

Roberta was a tremendous help and moved like a pro, stuffing items into the right-sized boxes. I was very impressed with her speed in getting rooms cleaned out. From numerous moves in her single life, she had the system down pat.

I moved in slow motion, accomplishing nothing. Everything I packed away brought me to tears. Each article I took in my hand brought me back to a period in my life with warm memories. I couldn't keep up with Roberta, who was doing ninety percent of the work. All I wanted to do was sit in a corner and pray for this black cloud that had engulfed our family to pass over us.

The weekend for the move was upon us. Friday night my boyfriend, Al, and I planned to stay overnight with my parents in East Falmouth to help with the last minute details. Leona and my mother were in the living room watching television together when we entered the house. My brother, Albert, was with Dad in his bedroom watching a Patriots football game. We joined Dad and the four of us cheered at each good play. I noticed Dad loved having his children around him. The loud excitement in his bedroom seemed to put some life back in him. The commotion took his mind off his illness.

The football game ended and Al and Albert moved back into the living room, leaving Dad alone. I stayed behind with my father.

"How have you been feeling, Dad?"

Looking washed out, he answered, "Not good at all. I've lost my energy to walk, and my freedom to get up and go anywhere."

Dad was worried and uncomfortable from not having had a bowel movement in five days. This was the first time he had ever spoken to me about any private issues. I tried not to make him uneasy talking about his complication. I gave him a few suggestions. I don't know how Dad had the strength to get out of bed and walk into the bathroom. My eyes filled up and a lump formed in my throat, seeing him so frail and weak as he walked in and closed the door. After ten minutes, he came back into the bedroom, and I could see his frustration.

He moaned, "It's so painful trying and nothing happens."

I got Dad comfortable in bed, left him for a moment, went into the living room and mentioned his situation to my mother.

She wasn't concerned. "The doctor gave him pills for constipation, and they'll work sooner or later."

I looked at her and replied, "It has been almost a week! He must have an impaction. If he does, the pills won't help him. He's going to need medical help."

I returned to Dad's bedroom and found him looking completely exhausted from numerous times he had tried again to relieve himself. He must have had terrible stomach pains. He wasn't eating much but that wouldn't prevent a blockage. I couldn't bring myself to walk out and leave him alone in this condition.

Mom went into the bedroom across the hall. After ten minutes, I realized she was settling there for the night. I walked into her room and found her tucked under the covers with no intention of going anywhere else.

"Aren't you going to join Dad?"

"I haven't slept with your father for quite a while now."

I stood paralyzed in shock wondering how she could leave him alone every night in their bedroom. Mixed feelings of anger and pity for her ran through me. My imagination went wild thinking about how many days, weeks or months Dad had been left to think about his life ending and suffering with his pain. *How long has she been doing this to him?* I looked at her, questioning if there was a heart beating in her.

"Mom, I'm afraid he might fall out of bed," I said looking for any excuse to get her to go sleep with him.

She replied back in an angry and demanding voice, "Go to bed and stop worrying about your father. He'll be fine."

I couldn't accept her coldness. She always used a certain tone to intimidate us so we would back off and leave her alone. This was one of those times.

Mom was trying not to face Dad's death. Separating from him protected her from the fact that she couldn't run from the end. At the moment, I didn't feel sorry for her because my thoughts were on my father who was sleeping isolated from his wife. *My God! How can anyone be expected to sleep with their own death imminent?*

I returned to Dad and could see the scared look in his eyes. I sensed from his tossing and turning, that he feared being left by himself. *Alone...*to think of your life slipping away from you, leaving your family, not to feel another human body next to you to receive comfort and security, not to have someone to talk to so your mind won't think about the death process. *Alone...*giving you time to imagine your body returning to the earth, wondering if God will find you worthy to be with Him in eternity, and the fear of suffering in Purgatory. All of these thoughts might have been running through his mind in the dark. *Alone!*

I went over and asked, "Dad, do you want me to lie with you for a while on the other side of the bed?"

His eyes looked like the weight of the world had come off his shoulders. Relieved, he said, "Yes, I'd like that." Peace seemed to flow over him when he realized he wasn't going to be abandoned.

Before settling down to rest beside him, I went into the bathroom. I was completely taken aback to discover that the room hadn't been cleaned. *How could I have been so blind not to know my parents needed help? Where was my selfish heart all these months?* Mom was in no emotional state to worry about cleaning. Getting up and facing the day was her chore. *God forgive me.*

The end was here and there was no time to make up for what wasn't done for them. Without knowing it, I did the same thing of which I accused Mom. I hid at home to protect myself from seeing Dad fade away. The same thing I did with Sandy. Another repeat. What I saw and felt in the five hours of being here couldn't possibly touch the heartbreak Mom had been experiencing day in and day out all eight months. It was almost midnight when I finished cleaning every inch of the bathroom, leaving it spotless.

When I returned to the bedroom, Dad had turned off the lights and was resting in the darkness. I bent to kiss him goodnight before settling at the corner of the bed. I placed my hand on top of his so he could feel the warmth and know he wasn't alone. This was my first real connection with my father. I stayed next to him until I could hear his last deep sigh of relaxation and I knew he was in a deep sleep. Hopefully, he felt safe and protected.

Morning came and the day was beautiful, warm and sunny. There was no time to take it easy and sleep late because the movers were at the house early. Family members were running in different directions, finishing what had to be done to make the move go smoothly and quickly. Roberta pulled into the driveway to pitch in again.

Camilla and Dante Picciano, Albert's in-laws, were standing in the kitchen after coming through the path in the backyard to see Dad. They knew this would be their final farewell to him. I greeted them and went to get my father. Rounding the corner, I couldn't see him in the bedroom. I stepped in a little further and saw him in the bathroom. He was sitting on the closed toilet lid with only his trousers and a white t-shirt on, stretched over the sink, trying to shave. The left side of his face rested on the side of the sink and he struggled to shave with the razor in his right hand. Never had I seen such a heartbreaking sight. Dad was determined not to bother anyone.

"I think you need my help," I said with a smile and a light, affectionate squeeze to his check.

He handed me the razor. I was slow and carful trying not to hurt him. I couldn't do a thorough job because his face was so thin that I couldn't get the razor around his jaw line.

I helped Dad wash and put him into the cushioned seat of a wheelchair that had been provided for him from the hospital. When we entered the kitchen, the Piccianos were no longer waiting. Mom had informed them my father wasn't up yet. I walked through the path to their house and they were nowhere to be found. Later I learned they left to do some shopping, thinking we would be there on their return. The chance never came because we left before they came back.

Mom was saying goodbye to the neighbors as I pushed Dad's wheelchair out into the driveway. Cathi Valeriani, who was the vice president of the Ashumet Valley Property Owners, Inc., had arrived to see my father. He had been the secretary for the association for three years. Since Cathi lived only a block away, she and my father would meet often to work together. I could see the heartbreak in Cathi's expression. Like so many who came to say goodbye, she wasn't sure if this was her last time to see him alive. Cathi's eyes filled with tears and she struggled to keep herself composed as she kissed him goodbye.

After all the farewells, we put Dad in Leona's car. Everyone choked up as we hesitated another moment for him to take a last look at his home. It was hard for me to hold back my tears in front of Al. I sat in our car and turned to face my passenger window trying to hide my wet cheeks. My father had to be fighting the same emotions.

The cars that had lined up slowly started to pull away. I turned one more time to look at my parents' home. I imagined Dad at the end of the driveway waving his hand high in the air saying goodbye. Knowing he would never do that again made me choke up.

Roberta was right behind us, with her car packed full. South Dennis was thirty minutes away and by the time we arrived, Dad was totally exhausted. The movers had ninety percent of the furniture in place. The house was a beautiful Cape Cod home in a nice neighborhood with plenty of woods around the sides and back of the house.

We took Dad around in his wheelchair to see all the rooms. At the end of the hall was my parents' bedroom. Two small windows filled their room with bright sunlight. Their canopy bed fit perfectly to the left of the entrance with the headboard centered against the wall. Their large dresser and mirror was on the opposite wall, facing the doorway, and gave the effect of the room appearing larger than it actually was.

I kept praying, "Please God, give Dad time to enjoy this place for a while."

Hospice

The following Friday night I returned to my parents' and stayed for the weekend. My first concern was finding out if the laxatives had helped my father. He informed me that he still hadn't had any relief from his problem. I talked with Joe and insisted Hospice should be called. Joe was uncomfortable with the idea knowing Dad was going to be upset. I was willing to take the complete blame. Leaving him in this condition was worse than him being angry at me.

Joe made the call. "Hospice will only come if Dad's doctor orders the service and if the patient agrees to their help."

"Give his doctor a call and see what he says," I replied.

Joe returned a few moments later. "The doctor is in favor of Hospice coming to care for Dad. The hardest thing is going to be getting our father to approve."

"I'll go and talk to him," I offered.

I went in Dad's bedroom and explained the calls Joe had made.

"Hospice will come to help, but you have to agree on their assistance."

"Will the procedure be painful getting the impaction taken care of?" he asked.

"I don't know, but you can't stay like this, because it's unhealthy and this condition can poison your system."

To my amazement, he agreed. I had no idea what changed his mind but I wasn't about to question it.

It was 8:00 p.m. when Joe called the doctor to make the arrangements with Hospice. They said someone would come to the house right away. Within an hour, I answered the doorbell. Standing in the doorway was a woman from the Hospice Association of Cape Cod, Inc. from Yarmouthport. Little did we know the stress she was going to take off our family.

She smiled with warmth, "Hi, I'm Cathy."

Her frame was so tiny that the tote bag in her hand seemed bigger than her. Cathy surprised me with her casual dress of sweats, and oversized shirt and sneakers. She looked like the girl next door and had a down to earth demeanor.

Cathy came through the front door carrying a handful of Hospice pamphlets and we introduced ourselves. I led Cathy down the narrow hallway to Dad's bedroom. He smiled and welcomed her. Cathy's glance back in my direction told me they needed time alone.

I joined the rest of the family in the kitchen. Joe, Albert, Bill and Leona were at the table with Mom. We all conversed, tense from the reality of someone from Hospice in our home. It wasn't long before Cathy came directly to the kitchen table to discuss Dad's condition. When she bent to open her tote bag, I realized she was pregnant. Her oversized shirt had hidden her condition.

She placed the pamphlets down on the table in front of us and suggested we read them when we had time. She emphasized that if there were any questions or problems, she was on call twenty-four hours, seven days a week. If she received a call from the family, she'd be there fast since she lived only ten minutes away.

Cathy then proceeded to tell us, step by step, what to expect as Dad's health declined. She explained the availability of services and detailed how their volunteers could stay with him to give family members time to shop or just take a break from the stress. The volunteers also would clean the house and bathe Dad.

We listened with no comments and asked very few questions. It felt like we were passing through a bad nightmare. Cathy knew from her experience not to throw too much at us or to overstay her first visit. She was wise to the fact that families had difficulty trying to deal with the last stages of a loved one's life.

I went in to see Dad after Cathy left.

He looked relieved, but remarked, "It was painful and uncomfortable."

"At least you'll start feeling better," I said hugging him. "When I go home Sunday, the trip will be easier for me knowing you're no longer suffering from a blockage."

The following Monday night I received an angry call from Dad.

"Why didn't you tell me the nurse who helped me was from Hospice? I don't want their service again. I'm not going to die and Hospice is for the dying. Why would you call them?"

"Dad, you must have misunderstood me because I was honest about where Cathy was from."

Please God give me the right words to say to him. I didn't know what was going to give him comfort about keeping the service. I only knew deep down all of us needed Hospice.

Finally, I said, "Dad, God decides who's going to die and when. Just because Hospice is there helping you doesn't mean the decision comes from them. If He wants you to live, you will." I continued, "You always worried about Mom being alone. If something does happen to you, Hospice will be there to help her cope. You make the decision. I was only trying to help the both of you, but if you don't want Hospice, I'll stand behind you."

God put the words in my mouth because my mind was blank for answers, since I hadn't been prepared for the call.

Leona had told me that Dad had cried in East Falmouth, saying he felt guilty leaving Mom alone. He was sadly aware of how much she depended on him and she was horrified by being left behind. I wanted him to keep Hospice, if for no one else, than for her.

In a defeated, soft voice he said, "Okay. I'll keep the service."

The Mystery of Walter

A new woman arrived from Hospice introducing herself as Debbie. She was going to be the private nurse who would be handling all of Dad's medical problems. Debbie told the family, "Never use the word *pain* with your father. Say *discomfort. Pain* will bring his mind directly to his cancer." Debbie decided it was time to start him on morphine. "I think you should administer the medicine, Alberta."

My heart was in my throat with the responsibility. The liquid medicine was to be placed under his tongue with a tiny dropper. I looked at the drug as a remedy to keep him sedated all the time.

Debbie placed a soft hand on my shoulder when she saw the concern on my face. "The dropper contains only 5 mg and this is the lowest strength to start. This amount will only take the edge off the pain and still allow your father to be aware of things happening around him. He'll be more comfortable and will be able to communicate with all of you more easily."

I became so absorbed with Dad that I didn't want to leave his side. I spent little time talking to my mother. Sharon and Maria, my sisters-in-law, stayed over every weekend and helped Mom. We placed two rocking chairs in his bedroom, facing him. I chose to sit in the large one because the rocker was his favorite seat when he smoked his pipe.

Bill and Sharon were expecting their first child. Emotions were high praying for Dad to hold out one more month to meet his fifth grandchild. Our father believed the baby would be a boy and talked to Bill about the things he could do with a son.

Albert's boys, David and Dan, were the only ones who would carry on the Gramm name.

Each day I sat in the rocker in Dad's bedroom, and I studied the picture of Walter that sat on his bureau. Our brother's portrait was a masterpiece. The artist drew Walter with wings. Why? Did he feel something before his death occurred? The image was a piece of artwork that left many questions and no answers.

Mom spoke about how Walter's picture became a mystery. She had taken Leona, Walter, Albert and me to a park in Worcester. A man approached her, explaining he was a photographer and wanted to take pictures of her children. At the time, Dad was in the Army and stationed away from home and she wanted his permission to take us. My father thought we would all be safe since he wanted her to go to his studio. She dressed the four of us up in our best clothes.

Mom said, "He seemed to focus a lot on Walter and did something very unusual. When the photographs were printed, there was one drawing of Walter done in pencil, and the artist drew him with angel wings. We never found out why this man saw Walter this way."

Mom continued with another odd occurrence. "I was ironing one day and Walter came up to me and asked, 'Mommy, is it all right to love God more than you?' I was completely shocked by the question and replied, 'Yes, you *are* supposed to love God more than anyone else.' After he got his answer, he ran off to play with you kids. The question left me trying to understand why he asked me this. His inquiry had sent chills through me."

It wasn't long after the pictures were taken in the studio when Walter got sick. We lived in Worcester, Massachusetts, and Dad had a meeting in Boston and decided to take the whole family and spend the rest of the day sight-seeing.

This is when Boston had an epidemic of polio. A week later, Walter came down with the disease. There had been so many cases that the hospitals ran out of iron lung machines. Walter wasn't fortunate enough to obtain one to help him breathe. My parents received a call in the early morning hours that Walter, at seven years old, had died. They were devastated for years.

My mother had a breakdown and carried guilt about Walter's death for years. Her regret came after she had spent a full day shopping in the city with Walter, Leona, Albert and myself. Handling twins alone must have been a handful, let alone with two other children.

Walter was being a normal boy and brother, teasing the rest of us. The event couldn't have been easy for my mother pulling four kids from store to store, and then fighting for seats on a bus while carrying heavy bundles. Mom was completely without patience from exhaustion.

"I got aggravated with him and said, 'I'll *never* take you to the city again!' I never did," Mom said sobbing.

The chance never came before he died. The statement ate at her and she couldn't find any peace because of the words she had said to Walter.

Dad went through the same conscience-stricken feelings with Walter's death. One day when he and I sat in the den in East Falmouth, he shared his own story with me. He had taken the four of us to a park in Worcester and was very upset with Walter, again for misbehaving.

"Walter had been fussy all day, and I got upset with him. I told him that I'd *never* take him to the park again."

I sat there watching the tears pouring down my father's cheeks with his head down in his hands, crying uncontrollably.

He looked up at me absolutely heartbroken. "It has been over forty years, and I still can't forgive myself for saying that to him. I never had the chance to take him again!"

It was the first time in my life I saw my father cry. It was a hidden side of him that he shared with me by exposing his emotions. I can't remember to this day what I said to comfort him. My memory of that moment was only seeing his innermost pain and heartbreak from losing a child. My parents took his death hard.

One other time, Dad confirmed a story my mother had told me about an event that had happened to both of them, some twenty-five years after Walter's death.

68

My father started his story. "We were in bed when your mother's face suddenly lit up like a flashlight was placed under her skin. I couldn't understand what I was seeing. After the light faded, I asked her what had happened to her."

"I heard Jesus."

"Did you see him?"

"No, but I saw a cloud at the top of the ceiling in the corner, and I knew He was in the vapor. He said to me, 'Let Walter go so he can come home to Me. Your tears are holding him back.' Our crying has been holding Walter from going home to Jesus."

I couldn't image the spiritual experience my mother had. What a blessing. Through the years, I had questioned her so many times wanting a description of what His voice sounded like.

My mother explained, "There are no words on this earth to describe His voice except I felt more peaceful than I ever had with anything."

My parents had mourned and wept for Walter until this apparition with Jesus. Since his death, Mom couldn't bring herself to go to his gravesite in Worcester. The visitation from Jesus helped her to gain the knowledge that our tears and staying in pain from a loss of a loved one keeps them from entering Heaven. The souls of the deceased want to comfort us instead of moving into eternity with God. Mom and Dad had to let go and trust in Our Lord to take Walter into His arms. He was now home and at peace. I had never forgotten these stories. Walter's name was rarely mentioned again because my parents had a difficult time talking about him.

Walter Gramm

Walter with angel wings

Walter in the yard

Dad and Walter

Leona and Walter

Saying Goodbye

Dad was tremendously weak and slept most of the day. My parents' military friends were all notified of the short length of time we had left with him. The couples started to come each day to say their final farewell.

A former General, who looked to be in his eighties and served with Dad during WWII, came to visit him. I peeked through the bedroom door that was cracked open slightly to make sure he was awake and alert enough to respond to his visitor. The man sat in Dad's big rocker with his back toward me. He was leaning over talking very closely to my father in bed, probably reminiscing about their times together in the service. Dad blinked his heavy eyelids. He fought to keep his eyes open in order to show interest in what the General said. Between his lack of strength and the effect of the morphine, he was in and out during the whole conversation. I couldn't understand how the gentleman wasn't aware of Dad's struggle to stay awake as he spoke to him. Maybe there was something that had to be said between friends before his passing.

Out of all the dearest and truest friends of my parents, one special couple didn't show up to see Dad. Joe and Anita St. Onge were so close to the whole family that, as kids and right through to our adulthood, we called them Uncle Joe and Aunt Anita.

Before the war, Joe had met my father when they both worked at the American Bosch Company in Springfield, MA. He joined the National Guard at the same time as Dad but served in a different infantry during WWII. After the service, wherever my father worked, Joe followed him to the same

71

company. My father retired as President of Pyrotector, Inc. in Hingham and Joe stayed there until his own retirement, ten years later.

Joe and Dad had a fall-out and never shared the incident with me. The two couples had to deal with a situation that separated them for over twenty years. Dad never talked about Joe without getting choked up and the empty gap between them was worse during his illness.

My father told me," Joe was a devoted friend, and I've been completely lost all the years without him."

Dad was an only child and Joe had been like a brother to him. They did everything together and as couples. Joe had spent a lot of years in the service with our father. With his days declining, Dad spoke to me often about Joe; talking about the old days. I could sense the mental strain and frustration Dad was under from wanting to repair the friendship before he died. The loss was so obvious and the love in his heart for Joe was tearing him apart inside. Dad wasn't in a position to make the call, so I prayed for God to give me the strength to get involved and do what had to be done.

Joe lived about four miles from my home in North Dighton. I had never stopped visiting him or my aunt because of the conflict. I made the call and told him, "Joe, Dad's near the end, and he really misses you. He's talking about you often. I think he longs to make peace with you. Do you think you can bury the disagreement so both of you can say what's in your hearts before it's too late?" I wouldn't be able to live with myself, knowing my father died without asking for or receiving forgiveness. I promised to be there when Joe came to visit.

"Can you give me a few days to prepare myself? I've known your father to be a strong man, and I'm going to have a hard time seeing him so frail and defeated."

Joe was doing the same thing that I had done with Sandy. His reaction made me realize how often people leave a loved one or friend facing death alone.

Four days later, Joe arrived, unannounced. He walked through the kitchen door, joking and hugging as he always did. I knew his teasing and wit were a cover-up to hide how awkward he must have felt in this situation. He had to have been very uncomfortable facing my mother after all the years of not keeping in touch.

When Joe came around the corner into the living room, my father was sitting in his wheelchair watching television. I don't think Joe got completely through the doorway when he broke down. He got on his knees at the foot of the wheelchair and embraced my father. They both held onto each other and wept.

The pain hit me hard, knowing two friends had wasted so many years because of false pride. One would have to have been blind not to see the love between them. I turned around and left them alone to say their good-byes. Dad was never told I made that call to Joe. My father was left with the feeling Joe came of his own free will. That visit had to be one of the greatest gifts for the both of them.

Camp Edwards Massachusetts Military Reservation
Training Base on Upper Cape Cod
Dad is in the front row, fourth from the left

Dad demonstrating the shooting position on the ground; Joe St. Onge gives the command

From Left: Dad, Anita and Joe, Joe Furtado and his wife, andMom

My parents seem to have a secret between them.

Dad passing out awards

Dealing with the Illness

I had been visiting my parents for a week, but it seemed like a month. Finding humor during Dad's illness was really hard to do. But one day the moment came without us looking for it.

Our father often asked to have his head rubbed because this brought him comfort. Leona was fulfilling his request as she rested on his bed next to him. I returned to his bedroom from the kitchen and stopped at the doorway. Facing me, the bureau mirror reflected Leona resting on Dad's bed in a deep sleep. Her hand was still in a cuplike position on the top of his head after massaging it.

She snored loudly, her mouth wide open from exhaustion, while dad slept. Not expecting it, this sight immediately struck my funny bone and I couldn't stop laughing. I went to get the others to share the moment to brighten our day. We all stood at the doorway, which made the scene all the more hilarious. Our roars didn't wake either of them.

Nights came and went and Mom still wasn't sleeping with Dad in the new house. I mentioned this fact to Cathy from Hospice when she arrived the next day because all of us found our mother's behavior cruel.

Cathy explained, "This is a very normal reaction from a person being left behind, especially with the elderly. Your mother is actually mad at him for making her face the last years of her life on earth alone and she's scared. She's running from the situation and is trying not to deal with the horrible thought of being without him. Try to be patient, and she'll come to terms with his death in her own time."

I started to be more understanding of Mom's neglect after Cathy told me this. I was so caught up in my own emotions that I by-passed her feelings. She was probably aware of what she was doing but didn't know how to comfort Dad without falling apart herself. I passed this information along to the other family members so they wouldn't continue to be angry at her.

Cathy found me in Dad's room each day that she came to check on him. "I'm getting concerned with you because I see you're not leaving your father's bedside."

"I want to embrace every moment left with him. As foolish as this may sound, I'm afraid that after his death, time would make me forget what he looked like. I want to have my father's face embedded into my mind forever."

She insisted, "You have to cut down the time you're spending with him. This is the time you have to begin allowing only two people at a time in his bedroom. You have to understand, the dying don't want to let go if they hear everyone around them. It's a gift to them if you let *them* decide when to leave you. Maybe you should make a comfortable atmosphere for him with soft music. This will keep your dad at peace with no confusion going on around him. You'll get a sign he's getting ready to leave when he starts leaving his belongings with family members."

When I told family what Cathy said, Joe and Marge went immediately to their apartment above the garage and retrieved their stereo system. In minutes the program was set up in Dad's bedroom and we were trying to decide what kind of music to play for him. Christmas wasn't far off so Joe decided on holiday songs. The first song he chose was *Silent Night* and my throat felt like it was going to bust from the throbbing pain of holding back tears. I didn't want to face the truth that Dad wasn't going to be with us for those up-coming days of celebration. *How are we all going to handle Thanksgiving and Christmas?*

To this day, the sound of Christmas music, and especially that song, brings an overwhelming sadness and emptiness in my heart. I have to walk away from people, whether I'm at home or in a mall, to compose myself. And at the same time, the songs bring him back to me.

I continued to notice how seldom Mom was in Dad's bedroom. Days would go by without her going in to see him at all. She slept in the spare bedroom and constantly kept herself busy cooking meals so we would all keep up our strength. Staying busy and out of Dad's room helped her avoid the sight of her husband slowly passing away. I didn't remember leaving his room to eat. The meals were erased from my mind. I couldn't cut down the time spent in my father's bedroom.

For a second Sunday night, I was leaving my parents to go home to get ready for work on Monday. I would return the following Friday night. I went into Dad's bedroom to say goodbye only to discover him in a deep sleep. I looked down at him and studied his face when a rush of fear came over me. *If I leave tonight, I won't see him alive next Friday,* I thought.

The feeling overpowered me and felt like a warning. I went into the den and in a state of panic; I paced back and forth like a lion in a cage. For the first time, I was losing control and my nerves were coming apart.

Marge came in and saw me in this condition. "Alberta, what is the matter? What happened?"

I started to hyperventilate, "If I leave tonight, I'm not going to see my father alive again."

She got upset. "What are you talking about? He's going to live. I don't want to hear this!"

She and Joe were still holding onto a miracle.

I calmly and lovingly looked straight at her, "Marge, Dad's dying! He's eighty years old with cancer all through him. You have to accept this."

She left the room in tears, refusing to listen to me.

I stayed the night and the following morning, I called my boss, Trisha, at Perkins Paper.

"Trisha, I won't be returning to work for two weeks. My father is getting worse, and I want to be here."

She was shocked and thought she didn't hear me correctly. "You're telling me, on a Monday morning, with this short notice, that starting *today* you're not coming in for two weeks?"

I didn't care at that moment if my position with the company was gone. The need to be with my parents was more important. I could get a new job. I wanted to be there to the end. I had no doubt that my inner feelings were given to me from above.

I felt guilty and hung up, hoping she would understand. My absence for two weeks with no one appointed to take my place would cause a serious disruption in customer service. I handled the biggest account for the company. Undoubtedly this would cause a lot of stress and extra burden on the other people in the department.

After the call, I walked into Dad's bedroom and noticed how he seemed uncomfortable with three pillows under him. They were causing his head to tilt forward awkwardly. I gave him my soft pillow that I had brought from home. The head support went everywhere with me when I traveled. That cushion was the only one that helped relieve my own pain from an old neck injury caused from a car accident.

There was a selfish second of hesitation to take my pillow to him because without that special headrest there was a chance of my waking up with excruciating, throbbing pain in both my neck and head. A hard pillow puts pressure on the nerves in my neck which also leaves me nauseated for hours.

"Dad, you don't look comfortable with all these pillows under your head. Let me get mine because it's very soft. Let's try and see if another one helps you," I suggested.

He looked up at me, surprised, when I took one of his away and added mine to the pile.

I tried picking the softest one from his pile to bring to my bedroom for my replacement. Dad gave a sigh of relief when I slowly lowered him onto the new set of pillows. To my amazement, without my pillows, I never suffered any pain. I believed that God gave me a gift, after I showed that I was willing to endure agony to give Dad comfort.

The Rosary

One evening, I sat in my father's bedroom with Leona, Marge and Maria, and we watched Dad struggle to concentrate on saying his rosaries. His eyes were closed and his fingers paused going from one bead to another. Even with his loss of energy, he was still devoted to the Blessed Mother. When my father fought in Europe during WWII, he promised that if She brought him home safe to his family, he would say a rosary every day until his death. He never broke his promise.

Leona leaned over and asked him, "Dad, do you want us to say the prayer and you can follow along with us?"

He looked up at her and replied in a frail voice. "I'd like that."

Marge and Leona disappeared to collect their personal rosaries. When Leona returned, she noticed that Maria and I had none in our hands. We both felt embarrassed and acknowledged not owning one and having absolutely no idea on how to say them. Leona searched around the house until she found two extra rosaries.

The Rosary is divided into five decades. Each decade represents a mystery or event in the life of Jesus and Mary. There are four sets of mysteries to the Rosary; *Joyful, Luminous, Sorrowful, and Glorious*. As suggested by the Pope John Paul II the Joyful mysteries are said on Monday and Saturday, the Luminous on Thursday, the Sorrowful on Tuesday and Friday, and the Glorious on Wednesday and Sunday (with this exception: Sundays of Christmas season - The Joyful; Sundays of Lent – Sorrowful).

As Marge and Leona took turns leading us through each mystery, Maria and I followed along. I was amazed that they knew the prayer by heart. Dad started to move his fingers along each bead and within a short time, he stopped and closed his eyes. For the first time in my life, I realized the rosary is a story of Jesus' and Mary's lives.

Catholic children received rosaries when they made their First Holy Communion and I was no different; but I never learned them. I started to wonder how many children are taught this devotion to The Blessed Mother. "The family that prays together stays together."

I had stopped my Catholic practice fifteen years earlier and had no desire to learn the rosary or go to church during the bad times in my marriage. I felt like God had abandoned me after all my prayers to Him. When my marriage with Richie fell apart, my faith weakened. I wanted to be a loyal wife and mother. I fought to hold my family together and maintain my sanity. I attended Mass every Sunday morning and took Debbie and Lori with me. I wanted God to be a big part of their lives. That was the way I thought, until my world came crashing down during one Mass.

The priest was about to serve Holy Communion so I stood up and followed the people in front of me who were leaving the pew to go down the aisle. My daughters stayed behind to wait for me because they were too young to take the Body and Blood of Jesus. For no reason that I was aware of, I started to feel smothered standing between the person in front and behind me. I tried not to become anxious by taking deep breaths and telling myself to calm down. I couldn't understand what was happening to me.

When the line started to move forward, my knees shook so much that I feared my legs weren't going to support me. I began to sweat and I could only focus on what was happening to me.

My first thought was to get out of line and go back to my seat but I feared doing so would bring the other parishioners' attention to me. To keep from falling to the floor, I held onto the end of each pew with my right hand. I had never experienced this before and encountered my first panic attack.

I finally reached the priest to receive Holy Communion and couldn't get back to my seat fast enough. My nerves were out-of-control. My hands trembled and my heart pounded in my chest. The nausea I was trying to hold back was making me sick. I grabbed Debbie's and Lori's hands and left before Mass ended. I felt only anger at God. How could He have done this to me when I was only trying to hold my family together? It took me years to realize that the stress at home was affecting my nerves, but I didn't understand that at the time. Richie and I fought often when he came home drunk. He would be in blackouts and I tried to control his rage so that my children would be protected from hearing and witnessing the constant battles. The up and down emotions affected me mentally and physically. I couldn't handle going anywhere for months.

The fear of having another attack in church kept me away for over fifteen years. After that I experienced the same panic attacks when I went into any public place or was pushed into a crowd. I suddenly lost my independence and confidence to go out of the house. If I could get in and out right away from a location, or attend functions knowing I could leave if I wanted to, then I could handle going out. Otherwise, I stayed within the safety of my home. After four years of going to private counseling and Al-Anon meeting, I learned that my body had been pushed beyond what it could take physically and emotionally.

Now here I sat, with family, holding a rosary. Our purpose was to say the prayer for Dad but I felt something happening inside me. I started to have the desire to talk to God while going to bed and while I sat in Dad's rocking chair watching him during the day. I wanted to continue saying the rosary by myself. I decided to offer up my sadness to God with losing my father.

When I was nineteen, Dad told me, "Offer all your pain, suffering, fear and disappointments up for the souls in Purgatory. They can't pray to God for their sins committed on earth. It's our prayers on earth that set them free. When we die, they'll pray for us."

To this day, I have never forgotten his request. I also say a prayer daily for the souls in Purgatory which starts with one *Apostle's Creed,* followed by an *Our Father* and *Hail Mary,* and a *Glory Be,* said seven times. It was one of many spiritual gifts Dad left me.

I read the book, *Life After Life,* by Raymond Moody, and the paperback told personal stories about people in the process of dying and what they felt and saw during their passing over to the other side. They all remarked about being pulled toward a light and sensed that if they went in that direction, they wouldn't return. The light was telling them about the need for prayers, forgiveness and love for each other on earth. Any article on a person's experience with near death fascinates me.

I had a similar experience that made me feel like I was leaving this world. Bob and Leona were invited to join Debbie, Lori and me for dinner at our home in North Dighton. Richie and I were divorced by then. I was eating corn when Leona said a joke at the dining room table and the remark started me laughing. I got up still giggling and started walking to the kitchen to get coffee when, suddenly, a kernel went down my throat the wrong way, and I couldn't breathe. It went down my windpipe.

Bob jumped up and came running behind me and crossed one of his hands over the other and started to push inward below my rib cage. I had no pain or fear at that moment and never heard Debbie on the phone next to me calling for an ambulance.

I remember swiftly and abruptly going into myself and had a sense of being separated from my body. The detachment put me in complete darkness, without losing consciousness. I had the sensation my eyes were looking out through cut holes in a solid, gloomy wall into a lit room. I had no feeling of having a body at all.

I thought, *Soon I'll see a light and cross over into the other world.* I waited for this next step to happen with excitement. Even though the others saw me choking, I didn't feel like my air was being shut off. There was complete peace without any fright and I was in a state of total tranquility.

At that very moment, I noticed Leona and Lori crying and yelling hysterically. My next thought was, *Oh, Lord, I don't want them to see me die in front of them.* At that instant, I came out of the darkness and saw everything normally. I was brought back to my surroundings, and was aware of Bob trying to help me.

It was a wonderful, spiritual experience. I truly believe my feeling of parting was the beginning of leaving this earth. My family said I was choking—I only remember looking for the light.

Preparing for the End

Al came to my parents' home in South Dennis and told me he'd made a deposit of five-hundred dollars into my checking account to help toward my bills while I was out of work and caring for my father. There were no words to show him my appreciation. He was a giving person and took care of anything that had to be repaired or replaced at my home. I held three jobs to support my girls and our home. If there was anything he saw the three of us needed, he gave it. I was blessed with this special man in my life.

God bestowed me with more abundance. Roberta arrived and delivered a card from my co-workers. They collected over four-hundred dollars from the employees, salespeople and the managers. God was surely taking care of me.

Bill and Sharon started to stay at our parents' house more often and Sharon worked in the kitchen to help our mother with the meals. The family worried about Sharon being pregnant and under so much stress.

The next day, my father called the boys into his bedroom and started to pass out some of his service collections. Dad gave Bill the German sword that he confiscated during WWII. Albert received Dad's rifle, the one with which he had won three National Rifle Association Marksmanship titles during the 1930's. He tried to give Leona all his service medals because she took them out so often to look at and study, but she felt all his Army memorabilia should be left to his sons and so the medals were passed down to Joe. Dad was now doing what Cathy said would happen before he would start to let go of his family and his earthly life.

84

The following night my father had difficulty breathing, so Cathy was called to come over to confirm that he was all right. When she arrived, she went straight to his bedroom and closed the door to have a personal conversation with him. I wondered how she performed this emotional work while pregnant. She never showed any signs of being tired or over-burdened.

Cathy gave us peace of mind when she came out of his bedroom and said our father was fine for the moment. When she was ready to go, I walked her to the door. The evening was a beautiful, warm night for October and the clear sky glowed with hundreds of stars. We decided to sit together on the front steps and just relax. She had given such support that I wanted her to know from my heart what she meant to the family.

I opened up to her. "Cathy, you and the women from Hospice are angels from heaven. Without the service, we would have been doing everything all wrong."

Their support taught us that there was no need for any family to go through this heartbreak and stress alone.

Each night we continued with the rosary only to see Dad's concentration leaving him. He could no longer follow the beads with his fingers; he would try, then stop and close his eyes.

By now, I had become aware of all the decades of the mysteries of the rosary. Knowing what the beautiful, holy prayer was all about allowed me to pray from my heart and feel the closeness of God that was all around me. I talked to Jesus not only through prayer but also in my thoughts during the daily tasks I did for Dad. I could feel God's presence and my strength was coming from a source other than myself; the strain was there but so was the comfort.

We called the Holy Trinity Church in Harwich to request our father receive Holy Communion every day. He had trouble swallowing and had completely stopped eating. One morning while Dad was taking Communion from his bedside, he started to choke. I asked the priest if I could take the Host for him.

Dad jumped right in, upset. "No, I'll take it myself!"

No matter how sick he was, he could handle taking the Eucharist.

With each visit, before the priest left, he gently placed his hand on Dad's shoulder and said, "Continue on your journey, Al."

I was heartsick knowing that at any time he could be taken from us.

The next afternoon Marge and I massaged Dad's legs with body lotion when we noticed his feet felt as cold as ice.

I placed the blankets on top of him and remarked, "Your feet are freezing, Dad. Let me warm them up for you."

He looked up at me and smiled. "They don't feel cold."

I informed Cathy with her next visit about the small incident.

She told us, "Stop massaging because kneading any body parts only spreads the cancer faster. His circulation is shutting down."

The family talked about her remark but felt that nothing was going to stop his dying process. Since this rubdown gave him such pleasure, we decided to continue, without saying anything to Cathy. After all, what other human contact did Dad have?

The next morning, Debbie arrived from Hospice, and gave Dad his daily examination. When she was done, she came into the kitchen to talk to the family.

Calmly and directly, she informed us, "This will be the last weekend with your father."

Her years and experience working with the terminally ill gave her the insight on what to expect and when death would occur.

Debbie started to explain what the medical signs were when a person was ready to pass away.

"His kidneys are shutting down and I can tell this by the brown color in his urine. That's usually what happens at the end. The last thing the dying loses is his hearing, so he'll be aware of things being said for a while."

Joe and Albert got up from the kitchen table and went outside. They didn't want to hear any of this.

The words made me so sick to my stomach that I thought the horrifying news was going to make me throw-up. *Oh, God,*

I thought I had a hold on this! I knew—we all knew—his death was coming but actually hearing he would be gone by the end of the week, brought all the underlying feelings of impending doom, to the surface. There was now a time limit placed on how long we had left with him.

I struggled to stay in control in front of my mother but I could feel myself unraveling. I felt dizzy, faint and feared a breakdown was going to shatter me into pieces. I tried to block out Debbie's voice in an effort to get a grip on my surroundings and control my emotional state.

I sensed everyone at the kitchen table felt the same way. Not one of us could give support to the other. When Debbie finished talking, she left the house and not one person spoke. We were all trying not to give way to our tears in front of Mom. Each person went their separate way to deal with their own denial and pain. Somehow, I got up from the table without breaking down and crying.

I was frantic now to hold onto every last moment with my father. I sat in his rocking chair for hours; my eyes fixed on him as he slept. This was going to be my last week with him. I didn't want to let go and couldn't imagine life without him.

As I rocked slowly, I studied his breathing. He was in a deep sleep. There was no music playing, no other person in his bedroom. It was a time for us alone. My mind started to drift in prayer, and I tried to speak to my father spiritually.

Dad, miracles happen, don't they? Remember us talking about them? God, don't take him from me. He's the frame to our family.

Prayers are answered, but deep down I knew his life was over and that God was calling him home. I looked at the drawing of Walter that sat on Dad's tall bureau next to him with the angel wings. *Is Walter waiting for you?* I wondered.

Without any warning, my father opened his eyes, gave me a warm, loving smile and held direct eye contact with me for a few seconds; the same soft smile he had given me throughout my life. His gaze went right through to my heart. As always, his smile said so much without words. He showed such alertness that it was hard to believe he was even ill.

87

I smiled back, hoping my love reached him the same way. He closed his eyes, giving us no time to converse. Little did I know there would never be another time I would see him awake. His smile was the most powerful gift he could have given me. This shared moment would last me a lifetime. My heart wanted to believe that he woke up to personally say goodbye to me.

Dad's Passing

Maria left Sunday night to go back to work at her hair salon and Albert was going to continue the vigil with the family. Maria would be returning the following Friday for the weekend. The same ritual I had had. As we said goodbye, Maria feared she wouldn't see Dad alive again. I tried to assure her that Dad would be waiting. I felt uneasy telling her that because I feared that she wouldn't see Dad alive again. She left crying.

Tuesday night, Mom told us that she was finally going to sleep next to Dad and that it was something she had to do. It must have been so difficult for her even though she had slept next to him for over fifty years.

By now, I had lost ten pounds. Waking up during the middle of the night was a normal thing for all of us and getting back to sleep was sometimes impossible. My body felt like it weighed a ton each morning. After only a few hours' sleep, family members connected in the kitchen frequently during the night.

Friday morning I woke up and heard the television softly in the living room. It was four in the morning. Walking toward the sound, half awake, I found Leona sitting on the couch watching the early morning shows.

She admitted to not being able to sleep. It was the first time during the week that both of us had had the time to sit alone and talk. Our conversation only lasted a short time, since we were both worn out mentally and physically. I started to head back to my room when Leona asked if she could give Dad his morphine instead of me. She said it was something she

89

wanted to do and Dad was due in a few minutes for his next dose. I didn't mind this one time and said goodnight at four-thirty.

Suddenly, I was awakened by a strong shake on the right arm. It was Leona. "Alberta, wake up. I think Dad passed away."

I jumped up and ran straight into my parents' bedroom. I glanced first to see where my mother was and discovered her sitting in Dad's rocking chair. She was absolutely still, making no sound at all, staring at my father. The low dim light on the nightstand reflected a very soft shadow on my father lying in bed.

I leaned over him and noticed that his eyes were open. My heart sank. There was no movement. This was the first time I was in the presence of a person who had just passed away. The event was terrifying enough, but this was my beloved father. My hands shook as I put them on his chest to feel for any movement. I then placed my hand up to his mouth and nose hoping to feel breath coming from him. There was nothing. I closed his eyes knowing he was gone...Dad was at peace.

Leona explained that after she gave Dad his medicine, she sat in the rocking chair to share alone time with him in the silence of the early morning hours. Moments later, his breathing changed; it wasn't normal. She sensed the worst and walked over to the opposite side of the bed to quietly wake Mom.

As my mother started to sit up, she rubbed both her shoulders. When she did, Dad looked over at her. Leona motioned for Mom to settle down with her in one of the rockers. In case he was dying, Leona wanted no sound around him, so he would go without anyone holding him back. As they sat together, Dad's breathing got worse. He had taken two long, deep breaths then stopped.

My insides trembled as I stood there looking at his body. There was no life in him. He was so still. I started to panic from the reality of death. The control I held for two weeks was falling apart. Why did he pass away in front of Leona and not me? Why didn't she wake me along with my mother? I selfishly resented not having had this private moment with my father. It was *me* who administered his medicine. This was the one time that I wasn't by his side. My heart knew deep down, he didn't choose anyone; God just called him. As a daughter, I felt abandoned by him, leaving while I slept in the next bedroom.

Leona went to get the rest of the family members. They were all sleeping at Joe's and Marge's apartment next door. Gradually, everyone came into Dad's bedroom, except Albert. He went straight into the living room because he feared seeing our father. I reminded the family that Dad might still be able to hear us and to tell him we loved him. Leona went to talk with Albert and he eventually approached Dad's bed. We stood around him, realizing he had left us forever.

Dad passed away on Friday, October 19, 1990 at 5:15 am. I was forty-nine and I felt like a child losing all my security. Mom stayed sitting in the rocking chair with a numb expression on her face. Cathy was called with the news and within minutes she arrived. She called the funeral home. My three brothers had made funeral arrangements a few weeks ago so they wouldn't have to deal with them when the time came.

Cathy asked if anyone wanted to help her prepare the body before the men from the funeral home arrived. Light dizziness started to overtake me again. Leona and I wanted our father to keep his dignity while being undressed so we stepped back. Bill offered and the bedroom door closed.

The overseers from the Doane, Beal and Ames Funeral Home in North Dennis asked if the family could congregate in another room. The director assured us nothing bad would happen, but felt we would be disturbed if any of us saw the body being removed.

The rest of the family went up the stairs to the attic on the second floor. There was nothing for us to sit on so we stood and waited. Multiple boxes from the recent move filled the attic. I wondered if the contents would ever mean anything to Mom again.

We all waited, feeling odd in hiding. The word *body* kept going through my mind. *Removal of the body:* that body was our father! He was somebody; he was ours. He was Brigadier General, Albert L. Gramm, Sr. *Please, don't call him a body.* I wanted to scream, "Refer to him by name!"

I was mad at myself for agreeing to be isolated upstairs. I had faced everything. Why not say goodbye to Dad? My insides raced. Foolishly, my mind filled with the thought that if I saw him being taken out of the house, it would be easier to face the reality of this horrible loss. I could hear the people talking at the bottom of the stairs.

For some reason, the attic door unlatched and started to open. It was just enough space for me to catch a glimpse of a shape inside a black, zipped-up bag on a gurney. *That was the image they wanted us to avoid seeing.* I closed my eyes and stepped back. I was warned and from not listening, I faced a gruesome memory. I heard Bill talking to someone from the funeral home and wanted to run down to join him, but my legs were frozen in place. I could only hear my shallow breathing.

In minutes, the moment for the last farewell was gone. There was enough time to go down the stairs to get a glimpse of the hearse as it pulled out of the driveway. In slow motion, it traveled down the street, leaving me with a separation that was tearing me apart.

Cathy gave her last condolences as we all gathered at the bottom stairway at the front door. It was the same location where Cathy and I had said our first hello. It was only two weeks ago but it seemed like months. She was about to walk out of our lives and move on to another family needing Hospice services.

Dad had feared dying in a hospital because he considered a medical center a cold place to spend his last days on earth. I thank God that he got his wish to be at home with all of us near him. He had the pleasure of seeing our faces every single day at his bedside and to hear our voices and sometimes laughter as we sat with him.

It was so final. The loving care I had given him for the last days of his life had been erased. Dad was no longer in the house and everything was quiet and still in his bedroom. All of us walked around in disbelief not knowing what to say or do.

We were used to being in his bedroom all day. Now, he was gone. No one was willing to face what had just happened.

I went alone into Dad's bedroom and sat on the edge of his bed where he had lain just an hour ago. The indent from his body still showed in his mattress and I rubbed my right hand over the area. I could still feel his body heat under the covers.

Leona entered the room and walked over and placed Dad's rosaries in my hand.

"I think you should have Dad's rosaries along with his prayer book. If you say them every night, in a few weeks you could learn them."

His rosaries showed the years of use. There were three cream colored beads missing from the twine rope. I wondered if he rolled them in his fingers during his prayers and broke them off.

Leona continued, "I want you to know, if they have been kept under a light for a while, and you turn the light off, they'll glow in the dark."

No gift could have meant more to me. I thought my presence was going to be a gift to my father, but now I felt he was leaving me a gift with his death...my faith. It was inside me again and I hungered for the closeness to God. In my own way, I knew my life wasn't going to be without Him or prayer. I just didn't realize how much worshiping would be in my daily life.

Leona reached in front of me and took my pillow off of Dad's bed, the one I had loaned him.

She bent down to give it back to me. "You can have this back now."

That action was the breaking point of my dam. The two weeks of being the strong daughter and sister came to an end.

I crunched the pillow into my face, crying with absolutely no control, sobbing and repeatedly saying, "I can still smell him on it! I can still smell him on it!"

The tears just rolled down my checks. Sounds came out of me that I had never heard. I have cried many times in my life but nothing like this. I felt separated from myself.

My cries were so loud that my mother came rushing down the hallway from the kitchen, still carrying a dish towel over her shoulder. It had been five hours after Dad's death and she had continued doing the household chores like nothing had occurred.

"Who's crying?" she demanded with an angry face. When she spotted me, she yelled, "Cry your heart out now and *never* cry for your father again! He's at peace."

She left Dad's bedroom immediately after her statement, so she wouldn't have to comfort me. If she hadn't left his room, her strong wall would have collapsed.

She didn't have to explain the importance for me not to cry continuously. I knew that her request stemmed from her experience with Jesus telling her to let go of Walter. She didn't want my tears to keep our father from going to Heaven.

My family helped our father move to another world with his life after death. He had become another soul in Purgatory who needed our prayers. This is a place souls go to for purification before they can enter into Heaven.

Our Blessed Mother has repeatedly said in Her messages to the world, "PRAY, PRAY, PRAY! Souls need our prayers."

So many times we all turn to God only when we need Him. I realized that material things aren't important. The people I love are vital in my life. God keeps trying to tell us, *"Love one another as I have loved you"* (St. John, 15.12). Dad's physical body has left me, but his love will live in me through spirit.

Maria returned Friday afternoon, heartbroken that her fear had come true. She missed the last opportunity to be with Dad by a few hours. In reality, all of us said goodbye to him, including her. Once he went into the coma, no one had a chance to say anything to him.

Cathi Valeriani called the afternoon Dad passed away. She had planned to come and deliver some wonderful news to him. The Ashumet Valley Property Owners, Inc. from the Town of Falmouth was planning a dedication in memory of him. The ceremony was going to be in East Falmouth right in front of my parents' former home on Fordham Road. They were naming the center island strip the *Al Gramm Park*. Cathi was so heartbroken to learn that the announcement came too late to convey to Dad. He would have been so happy.

The first night without our father fell upon us. The family stayed with Mom for the wake and funeral. I had another week before returning to work and could spend the time with her. I still didn't know how to unburden Mom. My heart kept telling me she didn't want to feel a soft hand on her shoulder or to be embraced. These actions would probably make her fall apart.

I entered my bedroom, which was next to my mother's, and could feel Dad's presence in the next bedroom. His death was only this morning. The silence seemed to echo throughout the house. No one was in the kitchen talking as we had been for a week. I felt the loss of Dad and became numb. It was now time to face his death. *You know it all now, Dad, with the life after! Please God, let him be at peace, forgive him for his earthly sins, and judge him by what was in his heart. He gave so much of himself to all of us. Let him be with Walter.*

I pulled the covers over me but no position was comfortable. I tossed and turned only to settle facing my nightstand. Dad's rosaries, along with the blue prayer book, were on top of it. I took the rosaries in my hands and held them but my mind couldn't concentrate on praying. My hurt and emptiness were too strong and painful at the moment. As I drifted off to sleep, comfort came to me having the beads in my possession.

I was abruptly awakened because my body was in the routine of not sleeping for very long at a stretch. With all of my tension and the exhaustion, I should have passed out until morning. I reached over to switch the light on to see the time. Only a half hour had gone by since I dozed off.

I got out of bed feeling drugged from sleep deprivation. As I crossed the hall to go into the bathroom, I passed by Mom's bedroom. She was in bed where Dad had just died that morning. I could hear her tossing and turning, accompanied by soft, deep, moans. I entered her room and didn't want to frighten her so I put my hand lightly on her right shoulder.

Bending down, I asked, "Are you all right, Mom?"

Her back was toward me as she half turned to look up, "I don't know what's wrong with me, but I can't sleep."

The tears filled my eyes. *You just lost your husband hours ago, and you're questioning why you can't sleep?* How alone she must have felt in their bed.

I whispered, "Let me try to help you relax."

I motioned for her to turn over to her side. I reached for the body lotion on her nightstand, the same container we had used to comfort Dad. I squeezed some cream out of the tube and proceeded to warm the salve by rubbing the cream in my hands before putting it on her back.

As I massaged the ointment into her back muscles, she sighed deeply. There was no conversation as I continued with slow, firm circular moves spreading the lotion from her neck, shoulders, and down to her lower back and waist. I was glad she wasn't facing me, because the tears were rolling down my face. I didn't think she had even cried yet, at least not in front of anyone. How I ached to hold her and have us cry together.

My mother finally gave a heavy moan and fell asleep. I pulled the warm blankets up to her shoulders and quietly left the room. I returned to my bed, and passed out from complete mental fatigue.

The Wake and Funeral

I was awakened Saturday morning with the sun penetrating into my room. For a few moments, I lay there and looked out the window wondering how a day could be so beautiful after such a loss in our lives. I compared the weather to a hurricane that leaves devastation in its path and, once it passes, the bright sunny sky returns leaving us with only the pieces to pick up.

Everyone assembled into the kitchen to pour their first morning coffee and each chose from muffins, donuts or cereal to eat. No one seemed to have the joy or lift to face the day ahead of us. Joe, Albert and Bill had already gone to confirm the final arrangements for the wake and funeral.

Hours later, they returned, with all the preparations completed. Visiting hours would be Sunday from 3:00 p.m. to 5:00 p.m. and 7:00 p.m. to 9:00 p.m. at the Doane, Beal and Ames Funeral Home in North Dennis. A funeral Mass would be celebrated at 10:00 a.m. on Monday at Holy Trinity Church in West Harwich. The burial would be at the Massachusetts National Cemetery in Bourne at Otis Air Base.

The family sat down at the kitchen table and Mom placed four pages on the table that Dad had typed up for us individually before his death. They contained names and phone numbers of those who were to be called. He listed family, friends, organizations, associations, including the National Guard service and the Social Security Office. He left Mom information on every single account they had together: credit cards, banks, homeowners and life policies, and, in detail, the phone numbers for every contact name. All the newspapers were added to the list. Who to see and call after

97

his passing were on the last page. I couldn't believe what he had done. We had nothing to look up. He stayed in charge, like the Brigadier General he had been, even for his final duties.

I needed dress clothes for the days ahead. I hadn't gone home to get any. Al offered to go to my house and gather up anything that was important for me to have. The effort to explain what to get and from where seemed like too much hassle, so I decided to just go out and buy something. The donations from work would help pay for them.

I went to the plaza a few blocks away from the house and went into the Dress Barn. I chose two white, silk blouses that were dressy. One was plain and the other had black trim around the collar and sleeves. I ended up with a plain, black, straight, polyester skirt.

I walked over to a rack to search for a blazer, in case the climate got chilly. The weather was still beautiful and the days seemed like Indian Summer in October. Facing me was a light jacket that had the same shade of black to match my skirt. I easily found jewelry to go with the outfits.

I walked up to the girl at the register with my hands full and placed the items on the counter.

Looking through the clothing, the saleswoman gave me a warm smile and said, "What nice outfits you picked out. Everything is so coordinated. Do you have a special event to go to?"

I answered, "Yes, I do."

Marshalls was next door, and I walked to the shoe department and found a pair of black high heels on the rack. They fit comfortably as I did a trial stroll around the store. I grabbed two pairs of black nylons before cashing out. What a blessing, purchasing everything with no problems. I grabbed my items and headed back to the house feeling satisfied.

As I entered through the kitchen door, Mom noticed my hands full of bags. "Looks like you got everything you needed," she said with a smile.

She asked to see what was inside the bags, trying to take a peek. I teased by pulling them away stating the clothes would be a surprise and I placed them in my bedroom.

The newspaper arrived and I sat down to look-up the obituaries. Someone else in the family had the responsibility of calling the information in from Dad's list. I couldn't believe the write-up. More shocking was the fact that Dad wrote it himself. I sat by myself and read the long obituary about him.

Col. Albert L. Gramm, president, CEO of Hingham from Dennis – Col. Albert L. Gramm, 80, of South Dennis, Massachusetts, retired president and chief executive officer of Pyrotector Inc. of Hingham, died Friday.

He joined Pyrotector in 1961 as plant manager and was instrumental in establishing joint ventures and subsidiaries in Germany, Switzerland, England, Australia and Japan.

Col. Gramm worked in the mechanical trades at Watertown Arsenal and General Electric Co., and was foreman of the Chelsea Clock Co.

He joined the 101st Infantry of the Massachusetts National Guard in 1928 and was inducted into active duty with that regiment in January 1941 as a second lieutenant.

While in Europe, he became Assistant G-3 of the 26th Infantry Division. By the end of the war, he was commander of the First Battalion of the 101st Infantry.

After the war, he participated in the reactivation of the Massachusetts National Guard and the Massachusetts Military Academy. He commanded the Second Battalion of the 104th Infantry Regiment, which was stationed in western Massachusetts National Guard.

Col. Gramm was a graduate and trustee of the Massachusetts Military Academy. He also graduated from the Army Battalion Commander and Staff Officers School, and the Army Command and General Staff College.

In 1947, he joined the American Bosch Co. in Springfield where he became manager of the Defense Products Division.

Moving to North Dighton in 1955, Co. Gramm was the branch plant manager of Tower Iron Works, assistant to the president of Anderson Aircraft Co., and manager of the Servotronics Division of the Standard-Kollsman Co.

He was active in the industrial organizations and was the director of several companies and two banks.

Col. Gramm was a member of the Lions Club, Rotary Club, Knights of Columbus, Veterans of Foreign Wars, Retired Officers Association and church organizations.

Born in Worcester, he moved to the Boston area in 1928 and lived in Hull 21 years before moving to Falmouth in 1982. He recently moved to South Dennis.

He is survived by his wife, Sophie (Dzengelewski) Gramm; three sons, Albert Gramm Jr. of Stoughton, William Gramm of Scituate, and Joseph Gramm of South Dennis; two daughters, Leona Waltman of Buzzards Bay and Alberta Lopes of North Dighton, four grandchildren and three great-grandchildren. He was the father of the late Walter Gramm.

A funeral Mass will be celebrated at 10 a.m. Monday at the Holy Trinity Church, West Harwich. Burial will be at the Massachusetts National Cemetery in Bourne.

Visiting hours will be 3 to 5 p.m. and 7 to 9 p.m. Sunday at the Doane, Beal and Ames Funeral Home, Route 134.

Donations may be made to the New England Home for Little Wanderers, 850 Boylston St., Room 3201, Chestnut Hill, 02167.

I learned about him through his obituary. He led such an interesting and important life and held so many high positions.

I felt distressed knowing the questions that I held inside would never be answered; they went with him.

Sunday arrived with the wake upon us. Mom was still holding up. We all gathered at the house waiting for the two limos to arrive from the funeral home. Leona's husband, Bob, closed the lumberyard so he could attend. Al was by my side giving me support.

Family filled the cars when they arrived. They backed out of the driveway, and my heart started to race. I didn't want to see my father laid out in a coffin. We drove onto Route 134 in South Dennis and came upon a traffic light that turned red: it was at the same intersection where I did my shopping the morning before.

A beat-up, blue Chevy pulled alongside of us on our right. A teenage boy tapped his fingers on his steering wheel to the beat of loud, rap music. I felt the strong vibration from the radio. He seemed to have no worries in the world. I watched as the other cars rushed in front of us heading down into the plaza.

My father has just died, my world has come apart, and no one notices or cares to look over at the two funeral cars.

My life had stopped, and I was surprised by how the crowds were going about their everyday business with shopping. For a moment, I wished for the impossible; I wanted to bring my father back into my life. My loss made it seem as though I was never going to be able to laugh and enjoy life again. Was this heavy sensation in my chest ever going to go away?

Within ten minutes we arrived at the funeral home. Al and I waited for the first car to empty before we entered through the front door. I climbed the steps and my breathing seemed to stop and my heart raced. Once we stepped into the front hall an overpowering fragrance from the mixed flowers made me sick.

Al and I walked toward the casket and my strength disappeared, my knees weakened and my body shook. The closer we got, the fainter I felt. Al took a strong hold of my right arm to support me. An Honor Guard stood tall beside the casket with an American flag. We knelt down.

I stared at my father who looked like a stranger. I looked around, disorientated, thinking we weren't in the right room.

"What's wrong?" Al asked.

"I think we have the wrong room. This isn't my father."

"It's okay, honey. We're in the right location."

I continued to gaze upon this unfamiliar face searching for something recognizable. There, on his right shoulder, was an Army rank braided cord insignia, along with his service medals. There was no mistake, it was my father.

The family blended into a receiving line when people started to arrive. Friends poured past us, not really knowing what to say to comfort us. Instead of our grieving family being consoled, I felt like we were trying to calm the people coming up to us. It was hard standing for a long period of time.

A stranger in line was now facing me. The gentleman looked to be in his late seventies and held himself proudly. He gently took my hand and introduced himself as John Hamilton. He had served under my father during WWII. His eyes filled when he mentioned the events they shared together and stated he had never forgotten Dad. With sadness, he described how bad the cold, freezing winter was fighting in the Battle of the Bulge.

"The military had problems keeping up with food rations for the regiments. Your father saw to it; no matter what was happening during the battles or where we were, he had a meal delivered to us every single day, even if the chow was a small portion. He was a great and wonderful man. I'm proud to have served under him."

I held his hands firmly and thanked him for making the trip to say goodbye to Dad. His story was short because others behind him waited to pass to the next family member. I watched as he sat in the front row, facing my father. His eyes never left the coffin even with all the turmoil going on.

I tried to stay polite while friends approached me showing their sympathy, but my eyes searched in between the line to watch for John. The physical openness from his grief only added to my own sorrow. John had gone up to the casket and touched the insignia on my father's shoulder. He had sat back down in the same chair, facing Dad. I couldn't concentrate on anyone talking to me.

John had positioned his elbows on his knees and placed his head into his hands. I watched as his broad shoulders shook. I hadn't missed seeing the devotion, respect and love from his gaze at my father. He straightened up and ran his fingers through his thin, gray hair to push the strands back. I saw him wipe his eyes with his handkerchief as he leaned back into the chair looking heartsick.

I told myself that when the lines thinned out, I'd go over and talk to him to learn more about my dad's life. I wanted to get his phone number so we could finish our conversation.

The mourners came in large groups and completely blocked my view of John. When the lines slowed down, I looked for the ex-soldier. He was gone without me having had a chance to join him. The chance to know all those stories went with this man.

A group from the Knights of Columbus arrived and lined-up with swollen pride. The respect for my father from everyone there made me very proud.

I glanced in a corner only to notice Joe St. Onge standing away from the crowd all alone in the shadows. I walked up and hugged him. His body was trembling. I asked if he had been up to see my father. He hadn't been able to do it.

"Joe, would you like me to go up with you?"

He looked relieved. "I'd appreciate that. I can't go alone."

I wrapped my arm through his and we both walked toward Dad. We knelt in prayer as Joe wept. How glad I was to have seen him before he walked out without saying his final farewell.

After the wake, friends and family came to the house. I watched Mom as she sat far in a corner by herself. People were talking and laughing without any of them taking the time to acknowledge her personally. Funny how people outside the family seemed to act like nothing had really happened. I know life will go on for everyone but having a partner had stopped for Mom.

The funeral was upon us Monday morning…the final day. This would be our last chance to physically see our father. I entered the funeral home and sat in front to absorb every feature of Dad for a lifetime. It seemed so unreal. After the priest said prayers, people were called to line up in their cars for Mass. I walked up to Dad and placed my hand on his. I couldn't bring my tears to the surface. I still felt like I was in a bad dream.

When we arrived at church, the Honor Guard was already standing outside along with the Knights of Columbus members. The Gulf War was going on and we were lucky to get an Honor Guard for the services. They left an impressive military atmosphere and it was heartwarming to see Dad's Army status being recognized. Seeing the men in their uniforms made me feel the absence of Dad even more. I pictured my father alongside of them. For so many years, he had attended the National Guard meetings in uniform. The sight of them lined up so proudly brought me back to the day when Dad had taken me to a Memorial Day parade in Rhode Island. At the time, I was twelve years old.

We had arrived early to reserve a spot on the street so no one would block our view of the parade going by us. As the different organizations, floats, and school bands marched in front of us, an Army unit that was out of range approached. I didn't know that the soldiers were from the 101st Infantry of the 26th Yankee Infantry Division or that Dad had been one of their commanding officers during WWII. They marched directly in front of us.

The Army's military band followed right behind them. The marching troops were ahead of the band, just far enough so the instrumental sounds from the company were at a distance. Their boots hit the blacktop with a loud shuffling rhythm. They marched in perfect unison and every step was in sequence with each other's. They stood proud and tall with their eyes straight ahead. The soldiers' demeanors exemplified their pride in wearing their uniforms with honor.

As the Army band came closer, the drums and horns vibrated deep in my chest and ears as well as under my feet as I stood on the sidewalk.

The whole atmosphere gave me a sense of these distinguished military men. Seeing them was a wonderful experience as I witnessed a branch of the armed forces trying to show civilians how proud they were to protect this country. Even at a young age, I understood this.

I looked up at Dad to say something to him while the group proceeded by us. I saw something I'd never forget. There was my father, in his plain weekend clothes, standing tall, saluting the unit going by while tears rolled down his checks. He stood as proud as the men who marched by him.

Back then, being immature and unknowledgeable about the pain of war, I thought Dad was being sentimental, remembering when he was in the service. Now, as an adult, I understand more clearly the suffering my father probably felt with the recollections of his fallen comrades. He had been in charge of making serious decisions for the servicemen in his unit.

It had been the first time, as a child, that I saw my father cry. Seeing him in such an uncontrollable state scared me. I had grown up feeling secure because Dad had been so strong in any situation. He never showed any weakness. Now I had seen a different side of him. To this day, when I hear a military band, it chokes me up.

Now at the funeral, the family assembled to go down the church aisle. My eye caught Trisha, my manager from work, and Roberta sitting on the right side. Their attendance warmed my heart knowing that they drove an hour and a half to be there.

My siblings and mother were ushered to the front pew as the Knights of Columbus members wheeled the casket with the American Flag draped over it. As Mass was being said, my mind didn't want to absorb the event. Deep in my heart, I knew God was giving all of us tremendous strength. Every one of us had been in complete control without any expression of grief or tears.

When the service ended, I walked outside to thank Trisha for coming. She gave me her condolences and explained she had to return back to the office. Roberta planned to come to the cemetery and brunch so she joined in the car procession.

One by one, people entered their cars to go to Otis Air Base. The Massachusetts National Cemetery is located in Barnstable County on Cape Cod, approximately 65 miles southeast of Boston and adjacent to the Otis Air Force Base.

As we ascended a hill on Route 6 by Hyannis, I looked back through the rear window of the funeral limo. I was shocked to see the number of cars with their headlights on that followed the motorcade. The family had been blessed with so many friends coming to bid farewell to Dad.

The cars entered at a crawl through the entrance of the black, heavy, iron gates of the military cemetery. *Oh Lord, I don't want to be here.* The limo parked near an open section with chairs lined up under a canopy on the lawn. The location was completely apart from the gravesite. Seven servicemen with rifles along with two Honor Guards got out of an Army van to stand at parade rest.

The casket was placed on top of a high stand in front of the family and draped again with the American flag. I looked over to my right at my mother. She looked pale. *How was she holding herself together—how were all of us?* I hadn't witnessed one person break down since Dad had passed away.

After the priest gave the blessings, he walked over to my mother. He bent down and whispered something to console her. Without any warning, the seven servicemen had started a rifle squad salute by firing three rounds, a military honor for a veteran. My whole body jumped with each overpowering, explosion from their rifles. *Oh God! My insides are coming apart. I'm not going to make it.* As the shots rumbled through the hillside, they echoed deep within my chest. I could feel the emotions buried inside me trying to escape. I bit my lip as the moisture in my eyes blurred my vision. Two Honor Guards took the flag off the casket and started to fold it in the proper military manner.

When the soldiers concluded the ceremony, one of them started toward my mother and gently placed the folded banner into her hands. I looked at her and saw a defeated women acting with pride. My heart ached for her. My love for her was more devoted knowing the battle she was fighting to keep control of her emotions.

At this point, I expected my mother to totally break down. Instead, she sat up straight, the honored wife of a Brigadier General. The pain in my throat choked me. *Please, God, hold me together a little longer.* All of us couldn't comfort one another because each person would have collapsed. We were determined not to shed a tear publicly. We were military children and wanted to show our admiration for our father.

The service ended quickly and everyone started to walk away to their cars to attend the brunch on the air base. Al sensed I needed this time to say goodbye to Dad so he mixed into the crowd leaving. I was the only one left sitting in my chair by Dad's casket. I walked over to the coffin and put my head down on it and cried.

"Oh, Dad, I'm so sorry. If only I had taken the time to know you completely. Please forgive me. I had so much to tell you. I love you, I love you."

Sobs overtook the two days of trying to be strong holding my emotions deep inside me. This was the last private moment with my father.

I don't remember the buffet or if I even ate anything. I just remember looking at the tables filling so fast and asking Leona where Dad was going to sit. We looked at each other with disbelief at my mental lapse. I couldn't fathom something like that coming out of my mouth. It had been a miracle that we both held up after my question. The brunch lasted about an hour and people started to thin out saying their goodbyes. The family members made their way to the limos and were dropped off at my mother's house. My father would no longer be physically part of our family again. We were left with our memories.

Again, we became hosts for our very close friends and family as they entered the kitchen where sandwiches, desserts and coffee waited. I sat silently as I watched everyone laughing and having loud conversations. When the last person left, we were wiped out and avoided speaking about the tragedy.

I had another week to spend with Mom and the events during this time were totally blank. For some reason, the weeks of Dad's illness and death were clear, but not the week afterward. I do remember spending days in Mom's bedroom wanting to be alone. There I sat rocking silently in Dad's over-sized rocker facing his bed. My imagination drifted back until I could picture him lying there under the covers. The bad moments were good: at least then, he had still been in my life.

The time arrived for me to go home and take on the everyday responsibilities of home life and working. Mom was left in the hands of Joe and Marge. Dad died knowing she would always be loved and be well taken care of by the two of them. I would no longer be making phone calls or having visits watching him run around the house fixing things. There would be no more pulling out of the driveway, looking back, and seeing my father waving goodbye to me.

Dad told me numerous times family was the most important thing in life. I remember him saying that a home is where you make your memories and not to fear the change of a new move. He advised me never to be scared of the unknown, because with any transfer, you grow. If you fail at something, just get up and start over again. He explained that each time he moved bigger and better positions came his way. If he hadn't made the swap with his jobs, his family wouldn't have had the things he gave us.

I went back to work knowing my heart wasn't ready to deal with the problems of customers complaining on the phone. The pain of losing my father was still fresh in my soul. I tried to work while fighting the depression. I wanted to be by myself outside of work. Employers don't sit and wait for their employees to pull themselves together after a loss. They have a business to run and money to make. I sat at my desk doing my job day after day with an empty feeling inside of me. From sunup to sundown, my moments were as if time had stopped.

On November 29, 1990, Bill and Sharon had a baby girl they named Olivia. Her birth occurred five weeks after Dad's passing. The date was so close, and yet so far. She wasn't the boy our father thought would arrive, but two years later on April 13, 1992, they would have a son, Brandon—another grandson to carry on the Gramm name.

Dad was thrilled Bill and Sharon were having a baby because they didn't want a family in the beginning. Bill had been in his forties and surprised our father with the news. Before Dad died, he was blessed with knowing they would have a child. Our father would have been so excited and happy to have little feet running around the house again. He had wished for more grandchildren to be added to the family, especially since he had been an only child.

A few weeks before Christmas, Joe and Marge had informed the family that Mom was bedridden with bronchitis. After work, I made the trip to South Dennis to see her. Being wintertime, the sky was already dark when I arrived. Unlike the other houses in the neighborhood, the outside of my mother's home had no Christmas lights to brighten up the yard. It was eerie. Christmastime had always been a big holiday and our parents lit up the property with decorations.

It wasn't that way this time. When I entered through the kitchen door, Joe greeted me and said Mom had been on medication but didn't look good. As I started down the hall to her bedroom, I glanced toward the living room. What an empty sight. There stood their Christmas tree; bare, with no lights or decorations. There wasn't a single gift under the tree. I remembered how we used to laugh with embarrassment about how many presents were under the tree: here we were adults, and we had more presents than most children.

I walked into the living room and stood staring at the tree. It was worse to see nothing on the evergreen than to not have one at all. Dad's death filled the house; I could feel him. Everything had stopped: not only our lives, but our spirit.

I continued my journey down the hall to see Mom. She was lying in bed, the same one she had shared with Dad. I bent down to kiss her and sat on the edge of her bed.

She was surprised to see me on a weeknight knowing that I had an hour drive to South Dennis.

"What are you doing here?" she questioned between coughs.

"I missed you and thought I'd take a ride to see how you're doing. Joe said you were not feeling well."

"No, I'm not," she replied.

Mom looked gray. I feared she was dying and was going to leave us two months after our father. I placed my hand on her forehead to see if she felt hot. She didn't seem to have a fever. I watched her closely as she talked and moved in bed. Mom didn't look like she had a serious condition.

"How are you really doing, Mom?"

Tears filled her eyes. "If only I could make a year, I'd be alright."

A year was so far off.

I held her hand. She was physically sick from the loss of her husband. Dad would have been there to wait on her. Mom's expression showed she could care less about what happened to her. Nothing gave her excitement, happiness, or even the will to go on. My heart ached for her. I let her cry and talk about Dad to clear the pain out of her empty heart.

At least my visit had given her some comfort. She had the opportunity to express her grief and loneliness to someone who listened.

Spiritual Signs

I was about to discover the many spiritual gifts left to me, even the ones from before Dad's death. The power of the Holy Spirit was stronger than I could ever have imagined; my father's passing made me aware of them. Everything started to fall into place.

So many mystical events had and were about to enter my life. I thought about when Albert had introduced the Medjugorje video to the family at our parents' home in East Falmouth; ten years earlier. He had told us that there was a Medjugorje newspaper we could subscribe to and that an author, Wayne Weible, had published numerous books about the apparitions. Leona and I had taken the address, intending to subscribe. I wasn't practicing my faith but strongly believed in God and these apparitions. I became too busy and forgot all about the newspaper and events.

On June 2, 1991, seven months after my father's death, the Ashumet Valley Property Owners, Incorporated, in conjunction with the Town of Falmouth, had the dedication for Dad. The main entrance parcel of the Ashumet Valley was named the *Al Gramm Park* in Dad's memory for his many years of invaluable service as secretary of the association. Cathi Valeriani, Vice President, came to present Mom with a plaque.

Our family, including the grandkids and our grandmother, shared in the day's event. Mom's mother was ninety-five years old and we were fortunate that she had the health to join us. Chairs were placed on the center island directly in front of their former home on the corner of Fordham Road and Route 151 in

East Falmouth. The moment was very emotional and a proud time for all of us.

After the ceremony, we had a family cookout across the street, in the backyard of my parents' former home. A year had passed since the move to South Dennis and the house wasn't sold. Walking through the vacant home and reminiscing about all the memories felt strange. When a loved one is missing, a place can be so meaningless. The emptiness resonated in the deepest part of me and it became more painful returning than staying away.

In May of 1993, I was finally scheduled to have a hysterectomy to remove my fibroid tumors. The procedure was held off for seven years and I couldn't wait any longer. I was having my surgery at the Brigham and Women's Hospital in Boston. The night before, Al was in my living room in Dighton watching television while I was in my bedroom packing my clothes neatly into the suitcase.

I had no particular thoughts going through my mind except trying to remember everything that would be needed for the five-day stay. Silly as it may sound, I was actually looking forward to being spoiled; getting three meals a day placed in front of me and having time to read a book or to say my rosary privately. Those crazy wishes showed me how seldom I took time for myself.

I was trying not to think about the actual surgery because the fear of being operated on would put me in a complete panic. I wanted to be brave in front of Al. At the age of fifty-two, I didn't want to act like a child.

From out of nowhere, I heard, "Do not be afraid. I'll be with you."

The words came from *inside* my head. At that very second, a current—an indescribably strong sensation—entered directly through the outside of my head and went through my whole body. I felt the rush enter through the top of my skull and the flow caused no pain. The feeling traveled with a speed I never knew could exist. The whole experience took only one to two seconds.

The impulse went instantly from my head to every part of my inner body and in one fast sweep until the tingle hit every limb, adding an immediate calmness and peace over me.

I stood there, in complete wonder and shock. *What just happened to me? What did I just experience?* This voice hit the deepest part of my heart.

I knew, without any doubt, that this was a spiritual experience. I stood there motionless; remembering only a peaceful, soft, male voice. I thought back to when Jesus spoke to my mother and knew this was now my encounter.

I don't know why I didn't tell Al what happened to me immediately after the event. How could I explain it? I didn't understand it myself. I was afraid he would think I was under a lot of stress before my operation.

I went to bed that night without taking a tranquilizer. When I had other surgeries, my heart would pound with fright so badly that I would be up all night. All negative thoughts would run through my mind on what *could* go wrong. This time, sleep came to me with ease and not once did I wake up before morning.

We were on the road the next day at 4 a.m. traveling to the hospital. I had to arrive by 6 a.m. Al and I talked and laughed for the whole hour-long drive without me even thinking about the surgery.

When we arrived at the hospital, I joked with the nurses and the anesthesiologist while I waited to be wheeled into the operating room. There was nothing but absolute calmness in me. I somehow pushed the experience to the back of my mind and didn't talk about the occurrence to anyone. I didn't know how to analyze the incident so I kept the episode to myself.

Months later, Al and I were watching a special television of people being interviewed about their spiritual experiences. A soldier told his story of being inside an Army tank during the Korean War. He had been frightened for his life, when he heard a voice tell him, "Do not be afraid. You will not die!" Then he described the same wave I had felt, going through his body and giving him peace. At that moment I told Al about what happened to me before my surgery.

113

"Why did you wait so long to tell me?"

"I don't know. Al, if I didn't understand the event, how would you?"

"Those are moments that can't be explained."

"When people talked about spiritual experiences like mine, I used to think they were crazy. I'm shocked that I was blessed to experience a miracle like this."

Al thought for a moment and replied. "God has his reason for touching us in different ways."

After ten years going together, Al and I got married on September 23, 1993. We said our vows in St. Rose of Lima Church in Rochester. The ceremony was a simple and private candlelight wedding during a week night. Al didn't want anyone to know, including our children. He didn't want to make our day a big event since we were together for so long.

I was uncomfortable omitting our families. We were extremely fortunate that our children all loved each other and both of us. Al's oldest son, Alan, was single and in his early forties. Lynne was in her late thirties, married, and had a son. Carol and John were still single, in their early twenties, and still living at home with Al. My daughters, Debbie and Lori, were both married, in their twenties, and had a daughter and son each. Al and I never felt like we had stepchildren; they were all our sons and daughters. I agreed with Al's request as long as we were married in the Catholic Church.

At first there were shocked reactions and disappointments from our families for being omitted from our wedding. Before long excitement spread and all was forgiven. Everyone respected our decision and held no bad feelings.

My home in North Dighton was sold, and I moved to Rochester. The town is a small country community with beautiful fields and farmland. I loved the area from the first time I traveled through.

Columbus Day arrived and my girlfriend, Rita Vasconcellous, from Westport, had invited me to go to her cousin's home in Lake George, NY, for the long weekend, with five other friends. Roberta tagged along with the group. The same weekend, Al's son, Alan, had tickets to see the Boston

114

College football team play in Michigan and had invited his father. The timing was perfect to fill my weekend instead of being alone.

The trip was worth taking just for the scenery alone. It was beautiful. A few hours before reaching New York, we stopped at a rest area surrounded by mountains. The women brought a "roadside" gourmet picnic of wine and shrimp. Rita placed a red and white plaid, plastic table cover on a picnic table. With a few laughs, good food, and an hour's relaxation; we were ready for the balance of the traveling time.

We reached our destination and each of us carried our own luggage. The large two floor home had four bedrooms upstairs and two additional sleeping quarters downstairs. The women were like children and tried to claim their rooms. We spent our nights, playing cards until the wee early hours of the morning. Laughter filled the house every day.

One afternoon we went to a small village just for shopping and browsing. Doris, a girl from our group, and I entered an antique shop while the others continued on into different stores on the street. I noticed a huge, old beer barrel that was filled to the top with holy medals. There were thousands of them to choose from in every size, shape and color. I had been searching for years to find a special one of the Blessed Mother.

There was one medallion that was...so different. The medal was gold plated, an inch long oval with a scalloped silver trim. In the center, there was the figure of Our Lady in silver. No necklace...just the pendant. The sign above the barrel said, "A dollar."

It was only a dollar! I turned it over only to see the name *Jerusalem* inscribed in the center. *Jerusalem...a medal made in Jerusalem.* I felt closer to Our Lady knowing it came from there.

How can I go wrong for a dollar? The worst that can happen is it turns black and I'll have to get rid of it. Another woman was watching me like a hawk patiently waiting and hoping for me to put the piece down. She continued to stare at the medal I was holding. Her action was what got me moving to the cash register. I held onto the medal like I had a piece of jewelry bought at Tiffany's. The pendant is still with me all these years and has never tarnished.

My mother gave me my father's gold necklace that he wore every day with a tiny, blue pendant with the Blessed Mother connected to it. I added my medal to his chain. The addition gave me a great sense of closeness to my father.

The dedication to Dad: The Al Gramm Park in East Falmouth, MA

Front Left: Bill holding Olivia, Leona, Alberta holding Meagan and Mom; in the back left: Albert and Joe

The Al Gramm Park

An Apparition

Not long after my trip to New York, my brother, Joe, called me to say Mom fell in the shower and was being rushed to the Cape Cod Hospital in Hyannis. He was sure she'd had a stroke because there was no movement on one side of her face and she was having trouble talking.

After her examination, the doctors confirmed a stroke and decided to have her transferred to the Joslin Clinic in Boston. I traveled an hour after work three times a week to visit her. Roberta accompanied me on my first visit, knowing I was upset.

Upon entering the hospital room, I expected to see Mom with serious physical changes from the stroke. She had no problem speaking and I was thankful there was only a slight paralysis on the right side of her face.

In addition to Mom being diabetic for years, the stroke had weakened her vision. She was now seeing double with the right eye and her right hand shook constantly. My mother was facing months of rehabilitation. She remained in the hospital for three weeks because her legs were now unsteady; she had to use a walker to get around.

It wasn't long after that, she had cataract surgery in both eyes, leaving her disappointed and frustrated because there was no difference in her sight. Being seventy-nine years old, diabetic, and having had a stroke, didn't help her eyesight. She wore a patch over her weak eye to keep from seeing double.

In 1996, I heard about a nun claiming to have seen the Blessed Mother in Medway, Massachusetts. Leona and I decided to take our mother for the hour and a half ride to the location so we could pray over her. We had hoped a blessing would happen and she'd regain some of her sight or hearing. This holy place wasn't yet acknowledged by the Catholic Church, even after miracles were received by pilgrims who had made trips there. A person could easily ride right by the location because there were no large signs indicating what was in that area. The entrance was just an open field with a path going into the woods.

Friends had informed us that the site was on Route 123 in Medway. We were told to ride very slowly and watch for an old, broken down, wooden fence on our right with a gate crooked and leaning on the ground. Next to the gateway was a small, scratched, white sign that said *Betania.* Leona finally found the site and she parked the car on the side of the road at the entry on the main highway.

We went in the middle of October, and there was an unusually, cold rawness in the air, causing us to wear our heavy, winter coats that day. Leona placed Mom in her wheelchair and wrapped a warm, wool blanket across her lap and legs. I buttoned my coat close to my neck.

We crossed the open field until we came to a dirt path that led through the woods. A short walk on the trail brought us to a tiny, wooden bridge. The shallow stream running under the overpass was almost dried up. The sight of the water only made the air seem colder, and a chill went right through me.

The atmosphere was so peaceful; the only sound came from the wind going through the trees. Blue crosses were placed in locations where people claimed to have seen Our Lady. The path suddenly branched out in different directions, confusing us as to which way to go. At the intersection, a huge boulder had holy statues placed on top. Pilgrims who had been there had left letters, family portraits, rosaries, and holy articles all over the massive rock and on the surrounding tree branches.

The three of us decided to travel up the path on our left. We could see a picnic table with two large statues of St. Joseph and The Blessed Mother behind it. This was the only section that appeared to have a place for Mom to sit and be comfortable while we prayed.

Starting toward the area, we noticed the ground was wet and muddy from a storm the night before. Three quarters of the way up the path we had to abandon the wheelchair because of it sinking into the soft ground. Leona and I couldn't budge the gear. We both supported my mother under her arms and helped her walk to the table.

After settling our mother, we noticed another deeper stream nearby. I had heard stories about people taking water from the brook and being healed from their illnesses. We had brought plastic, gallon milk jugs and started filling them with what we believed to be holy water.

We went back to join Mom at the table and noticed she already had her rosary beads in her hands. Within a few minutes, she needed to use a restroom. Directly across from us on the other side of the path, about forty feet away, was a small shed, which I hoped had a restroom.

I supported her by the hand as we walked across to the shack. The windows had wood across them so I couldn't see what was inside the building. I completed a full circle around the hut, hoping to see a door so we could enter. The structure was locked up tight and I was now faced with what to do for her. The walk back to the car was too long to drive her somewhere.

The next step was to find out if the three of us were alone in the area. People were always arriving to pray. I didn't want to be surprised by anyone coming upon us unexpectedly and embarrassing my mother. So far, we were the only ones in the area.

With the section being entirely wide open, I could see all the way down the path we had just traveled up. There was no doubt, no one was in sight. The entrance was also visible from a distance, and if someone was coming, we would have plenty of time to spot them. Three sides of the shed were surrounded by marshland, so it would be *impossible* anyone could come through the swamp. We were totally alone. There was only one way in and one way out.

Leona was across the path sitting at the picnic table and she watched in case she spotted a new arrival. My sister yelled

119

back to me that no one was anywhere in sight. It took only seconds for Mom to complete her task.

Out of the blue, a woman *stepped* from around the corner of the tiny shed only a few feet from us. You have to understand that I had just walked around the construction, and no one had been there! She would have to come up the path to get to our location. Leona would have seen her and it's inconceivable that anyone could reach our area that fast.

When the three of us came up the path, leaves, branches and twigs were all over the ground and our boots made a crunching, snapping sound when we had walked over the debris. Our movement had echoed through the woods so no one could have possibly walked on the path without making any noise. The woman walked right by me and headed straight toward my mother, like I was utterly invisible. Not once did she look embarrassed or shocked, seeing why we were at the shed.

As the stranger reached out to balance my mother by the elbow, she asked, "Can I help you?"

The woman, without waiting for a reply from my mother, proceeded to lead her back to the picnic table toward Leona with me following behind. *How did she even know my mother was handicapped and needed help?*

Mom's mouth dropped open, wondering who this woman was and where she had come from. The stranger helped Mom sit down at the picnic table, while I questioned Leona on how this woman came up the path when we both had confirmed no one was in the area.

My sister answered, "This woman *didn't* come up that path. I was watching the whole time. She didn't come from anywhere...*she just appeared.*"

"Leona, I walked around the shed seconds before, and no one was present. It's all wetland. There's no way, she came through that area!"

The woman placed herself at our table without an invitation and said, "My name is Miriam, and I come here to help people pray."

120

She looked to be in her early forties and was soft spoken. There was a very peace-loving way about her. She was dressed no differently than anyone coming into the woods and was wearing a pair of slacks and a warm, winter coat.

Leona sat next to Mom. Miriam was on the right side of Leona and directly opposite of me. She asked if we wanted to say the rosary with her.

My mother, who is outspoken, answered, "We can say our own rosary."

Mom was upset feeling like this woman forced herself on us and wasn't leaving. I was starting to feel differently because this was an unusual event, but I didn't understand what was happening. There was no conversation from Miriam like strangers normally have when you first meet. She didn't care to know anything about us, nothing! Her actions felt like she had been expecting us and was waiting.

Miriam reached over the picnic table and took my hands, asking me to join her in prayer. She never took her eyes off me. Her gaze went directly into my heart, like a spear, making me feel so much love. Mom and Leona finally joined hands with us. The two large statues of The Blessed Mother and St. Joseph were facing me but directly behind the three of them. Miriam started saying the *Our Father* and *Hail Mary* and we proceeded to follow along with her. I closed my eyes to concentrate and ask Jesus to hear my request for my mother. Then a strong feeling came over me to pray; not just by saying words, but to feel them from the deepest part of my soul.

While my eyes were still shut, I automatically took over and repeated one prayer right after another without stopping. I was so filled with passion that I started to cry and tears flowed down my face. I was so immersed in the consciousness of love and so deep in worshiping that I lost the feeling of being on Earth. When my eyes opened, I had to look around to remind myself where I was. My body felt like I had been floating and there was no connection to anyone at the table.

I looked up at the trees in front of me and the leaves were all in a vibrant gold. I gazed upon the two statues and their faces where encircled with haloes of golden glow.

I cried out to everyone, "Look. Everything's gold!"

Leona and Mom turned to study the space I pointed at. They couldn't see what I saw. Leona said she saw some gold on Mom's right hand which had been damaged by the stroke.

Miriam never once took her eyes off me or turned around to see what I was talking about which would have been the normal thing to do. I looked across to see Miriam's reaction only to find she was staring directly at me with a smile of satisfaction. She wasn't the least bit shocked or interested in what I was witnessing. From her continuous stare, I had no doubt she already knew this was going to happen. Oddly Miriam didn't want to mention the event or talk about the miracle. Her smile went right through me and I sensed a great affection from her. The connection was so strong, I would have spent a long time praying with her had I been alone. There was a mystery all around her. She hadn't been surprised that I saw gold.

Miriam didn't say the rosary. That was supposed to be the reason for her being there. Once I witnessed the gold, she got up and said she had to leave. She went over to my mother and gave her a hug before leaving. Her presence only lasted about ten or fifteen minutes.

The three of us sat in silence as we watched Miriam walk down the path that we had come up. She stopped at Mom's wheelchair, looked up at the sky, and then lifted her arms up high like she was offering herself up to God. We watched her in complete wonder, trying to understand what she was doing.

At this *exact* moment, Leona's rosaries fell off the picnic table. When she bent down to pick them up from the ground, our attention went away from Miriam.

We watched Leona pick up the rosaries, and in *seconds,* looked back again to see what Miriam was doing. *She was gone*! Disappearing so fast wasn't humanly possible and she couldn't have gone down the path with such speed. The trail was too long. Miriam had vanished as suddenly as she had arrived.

Mom looked at the two of us and asked, "What just happened? What did we just witness?"

The three of us knew that what had just happened was an act from heaven. I truly believe that dropping Leona's rosaries was planned in order to take our attention from Miriam's disappearance.

Leona asked me, "Do you know who Miriam is?"

"No. Who?" I asked.

She choked up, "Miriam is the name of Mary in Hebrew!"

"Leona, are you saying you believe that was our Blessed Mother?"

"Alberta, what just happened to us wasn't normal."

"I won't even argue that point. Something spiritual happened. This woman wasn't from Earth. Every visionary claimed Our Lady appeared to them as she really is so I truly believe we had had an encounter with an angel," I remarked.

That would explain the feelings I was having during the prayers. One hears about these appearances but we don't ever expect to experience them. We were specially blessed. Dad told me to open my eyes to things happening around me and this was one of those days. Encountering Miriam was a miracle never to be explained but only witnessed as a gift from above.

Our strange phenomenon had been one of many apparitions at Medway. Other pilgrims, who had visited the shrine, had claimed the sun would spin and turn colors or had witnessed the same gold throughout the wooded area. A blue cross was placed wherever someone had witnessed an apparition with Our Lady.

In September of 1998, another blessed event happened at the same location. Maria Esperanza, who had been considered to be one of the greatest mystics of our time, went to the shrine in Medway to pray with her husband, George, and other members of the Bianchini family. She believed in the existence of realities beyond human comprehension through apparitions with Jesus.

Maria lived in Venezuela and often had stigmata experiences, which is bleeding of the hands. Stigmata are wounds or marks on a person resembling the five wounds (two hands, the feet, and in Jesus' right side) received in His crucifixion. Maria told the staff of the Marian Messengers in Medway that when she arrived in front of the Statue of Our Lady, something beautiful happen to her.

While she was praying, Jesus appeared to her and said, "Tell members of the Marian Community that they need to build some kind of protection for the Image of My Mother on the land at Medway. Her image needs to be protected from the elements. When this is done, My Mother will open her arms wide and embrace those who come to pray and give them new hope and miracles will happen."

Sister Margaret from the Marian Community contacted Mr. James Merloni, the coordinator for the Labormen's Working Camp in Hopkinton to inquire about building a grotto on the land. In less than three weeks, the grotto was completed thanks to Mr. and Mrs. James Merloni, their son, James and Mr. Ray Conti, the stone mason who came out of retirement to build "Our Lady's Protection."

On October 20, 1998, Fr. Tom DilLorenzo, blessed the grotto in Medway. Ivan Dragicevic, one of the six visionaries from Medjugorje, in Bosnia had attended the blessing and had his daily apparition at the grotto site with Our Lady. Ivan married Laureen Murphy, who is a former beauty queen from Boston, Massachusetts, and lives six months out of the year here in the United States to be close to his wife's family.

** Since my writing about my holy experience in Medway, Massachusetts, the Marian Community, Inc. has been built on this exact location. To learn more go to The Betania II Marina Center, 154 Summer Street, Medway, MA 02053, Telephone 508-533-5377, website: http://betania2.com,

Medway, Massachusetts

A Blue Cross symbolizes where Our Lady Appeared

The Statue of Our Lady and St. Joseph

The stream and more crosses on trees

Searching for Answers on Medjugorje

After having had this experience in Medway and nine years after Albert introduced me to the Medjugorje apparitions, I began to long for any book about the apparitions happening in the tiny village. I felt a power beyond my control was calling me in this direction. Too many things were occurring in my life that couldn't be explained. I wanted to learn as much as possible about the apparitions of Our Lady seen by the six children.

The desire to have God in my life was stronger than ever. I became conscious of the fact that He waited patiently and lovingly for souls to turn to Him. When I opened myself up completely to God during Dad's illness, I came into my own spirituality. I *wanted* God in my life and began to realize, He *was* my life.

I slowly renewed my religious beliefs. Our parents brought my siblings and me up as Catholics and encouraged us to worship. Maybe my parents' prayers were being answered.

One Sunday, Leona and I decided to go to the LaSalette Shrine in Attleboro for confession and to just meditate. We were always close and shared our faith; we could talk about our religion for hours. I wanted Al to join us, but he had no interest in going to the shrine.

He said, "Alberta, go and pray. It's not my thing."

When I started going back to church myself, I prayed constantly for Al to convert. He believed in God but didn't want to put the effort out to go to Mass. One Sunday after I had attended Mass at St. Rose of Lima in Rochester, I came home and told him someone asked for him.

126

Surprised, he asked, "Really, who?"

I replied with a smile, "God!"

The guilt strategy and humor didn't work. Al continuously told me that he believed and didn't need to go to church. He felt there was no need to go to a priest for forgiveness. His belief was that he could admit his sins directly to God. Catholics forget that God gave the priests the right to forgive our sins. If they forgive, God forgives. This is a powerful connection with priests to Our Savior.

After Leona and I went to confession, lit candles, and prayed, we headed straight to the gift store. We went our separate ways in the book section, searching out what interested each of us.

I was amazed how much was written on Medjugorje. The numerous books on the apparitions made me realize how many years had gone by since I heard about this event.

I didn't know which book to pick up first. Then in front of me, was *Medjugorje the Message,* by Wayne Weible; the same author that ran the newspaper. I opened the book and started to read through some pages. The pictures inside were the selling point. I wanted to see what the little town looked like. I went up to the counter with religious articles along with my book. My sister and I spent the rest of the day walking the grounds. I thought back to the family helping Dad through his journey at this location before he had died.

I came home excited to jump right into reading. Waiting until after supper was torture. After the kitchen was spotless, I got comfortable in the corner of the couch with my pillow and picked up my book. Just looking at the cover and seeing the title *"Medjugorje"* made my heart leap. The anticipation of turning the first page was worth waiting for. I knew in my heart this book wasn't only going to be special but important.

Page after page had me so mesmerized that I couldn't put down the paperback. I grabbed onto every word, pictured every event and location, and studied each visionary's life. My imagination made me feel like I was right in this village and belonged there.

Before I realized the time, it was eleven in the evening. I knew when the alarm went off at 6 a.m. that I would be tired for work. After shutting the light off and pulling the covers over me, I went into a deep sleep, dreaming of this little village on the other side of the world.

I spent every evening reading my book on the sofa. My mind drifted until I imagined making a trip to Medjugorje but knew a trip like that was definitely out of the question. There was no way that I could ever go out of the country by myself, let alone fly that length of time. I had a terrible fear of flying and the few times I had flown in the past, was because it was my only option. It was a relief when I reached a destination, but the flights were stressful. My knuckles would be white on our arrival.

I thought maybe Al would go with me. An hour at church wasn't in his life so why would I think he would go on a pilgrimage for ten days that included church, masses, confessions, priests, rosaries, and praying? Al wanted us to go to Hawaii instead. He said spending a week with holy events wasn't his idea of a vacation.

Still, I couldn't stop reading the Medjugorje book. I spent every spare moment flipping through the pages. The emptiness and loss of not having more to learn about this village left me feeling unfulfilled. I couldn't believe this uncontrollable yearning to become more educated on this event.

I talked to the girls at work about Medjugorje every chance I had. A fellow worker in the warehouse was in the National Guard and had just returned from there. His position in the service was to keep peace over there. Employees crowded around him to hear his stories but I had no spare time to join them.

After weeks of not having more to read about on Medjugorje, Leona and I decided to go back to the shrine. I wanted to understand the visionaries' inner feelings seeing Our Lady. I wondered how many people in this world weren't even aware of this event. I was sure there were those who knew and ignored or laughed at the supernatural occurrence.

I rushed back to the book section at the gift store at LaSalette and found *Medjugorje the Mission* by the same author. This time I picked up a video named *The Mother of God Comes to Medjugorje.*

How could I be so lucky to find this? Now I can feel like I'm there in heart and spirit to witness the sights.

I couldn't say goodnight to Leona fast enough and drive home. I thought shopping for clothes was wonderful but here I was grasping onto something religious with more gratification than material things. I had purposely left the first book on the end table by Al's recliner hoping to tempt him to pick up the paperback.

One evening, he stunned me after saying he was already in the process of reading my book. I didn't want to make too much of his interest and prayed he would want to go with me to Medjugorje.

After a short time, I casually said to Al, "Imagine being on the same spot at the same time where the Blessed Mother is actually appearing to the children. I can't even comprehend the blessing."

He took a deep breath and said, "I would have absolutely no interest in making a trip like that."

His reply broke my heart. I hoped he would at least think about the pilgrimage.

I read the second book with the same degree of anticipation with which I read the first book. I held onto every word. I experienced the same sadness and emptiness when I finished this second book. I couldn't understand why this incident was taking over every waking moment of my life. A book never did this to me. The phenomenon was happening in another country. It should have been just a story to read about…not inspiration to jump on a plane and go over there to participate in the wonder. The thought of traveling to Medjugorje was so strong but I knew the trip would only happen if Al went with me. If not, the desire would be left as a dream. I felt foolish thinking so often about making the journey.

When our favorite television shows were on, I couldn't concentrate on them. I daydreamed about climbing to the top of Cross Mountain and imagined walking around the location and seeing everything shown in the book. You'd think I was going to be quizzed on this. If I had such enthusiasm with my studies in high school, my grades would have soared.

Al didn't have the slightest curiosity in seeing the video I bought. The weekend came and I put the tape on while he was involved with the yard work outside. I had no intention of moving from my spot until the movie ended. The film started out by showing a priest named Father Joe Whalen, who led the pilgrimage to Medjugorje along with a tour guide, Charlie Toye of Reading, Massachusetts.

I listened closely as the visionaries spoke about Heaven, Purgatory and Hell. The description was both frightening and captivating at the same time. The visionaries, Vicka and Jakov, talked for a half hour about Our Lady taking them physically to these three locations. I tried to imagine what they had witnessed.

I was learning about all these apparitions and wanted to stand on top of a mountain and scream to everyone that this was going on in our world. I wanted them to be aware of the Blessed Mother appearing on this Earth. I wanted others to feel the same excitement that I was experiencing. So much crime goes on in this world and people are turning away from God. I couldn't understand why the priests at Mass weren't talking about Medjugorje. The happening wasn't ever mentioned on television or in the newspapers. I had to stop and think, *Alberta, you were blind for years yourself!*

Two books and a video were completed, and I still sat each night with a far away feeling. Nothing I accomplished seemed like fun or had any importance to me. My interest in television was gone.

Why is this so important to me? A book is a book. Why is this one getting deeper and deeper inside my heart?

Meeting Arlene Albert

I took one more trip to the shrine with Leona to see if something else about Medjugorje could be found. When I reached the book section, I saw another woman searching the same area. She was a very attractive blonde, in her early sixties, and dressed in a stylish long, tan trench coat. We caught each other's eye and introduced ourselves. She had a friendly smile, was soft spoken, and seemed very outgoing. There was an instant connection when we started talking.

She introduced herself as Arlene Albert from West Warwick, Rhode Island. She was looking for books on Medjugorje, so I mentioned the two I had just finished reading. By now I felt like an expert on these apparitions and wanted to help her. Not long into our conversation, I realized she knew more about this than I did. I asked if she ever took a trip to Medjugorje. When she said yes, my heart skipped just to think I was in the presence of someone who had actually been there.

Arlene gave me some insight into Medjugorje. I got pulled into her story when she described miracles that had happened to other pilgrims, the peace in the village, the apparitions, and the miracle of the sun.

Arlene offered Leona and me a medal which she had bought during her trip. The medallion which was blessed in Medjugorje was of the Blessed Mother and the six visionaries at her feet. Having such a gift filled my eyes with tears. Just knowing the pendant came from Medjugorje was a blessing all its own.

"I'm planning on going back to Medjugorje next May. Would you and Leona want to come?" Arlene asked. "The miracles you see there are beyond words."

I thanked her but explained my fear of flying and of going such a distance. She promised to keep in touch with me. We exchanged telephone numbers and addresses.

Twenty minutes before, we were strangers, and now I felt an incredible desire to know more about Arlene. I never really believed she'd call me.

Surprisingly, Arlene and I kept our word and called each other now and then. I told Al about her asking me to go on the trip with her the next year.

He said, "Go, if you want. It's something you have been talking about for a long time."

I asked him again if he would go with me. He had no intentions of changing his mind. I had his approval and felt completely on my own. I had to be crazy to even think about going on a trip out of the country—not only without Al, but with a complete stranger. It was only August of 1997, and May was long way off. I felt there was no need to give her an answer right away.

With each phone call from Arlene, she would describe, in detail, the village blessed by Our Lady. I was filled with a combination of wanting to be there and the terror of flying. Whether I was at work, home or doing errands, my mind was totally on this trip.

Why am I being so immature about making a decision? What's pulling at my heart to go there after reading about the apparitions?

My mind raced with everything that could go wrong. I learned how much I feared doing things alone. Arlene was a woman who seemed nice and our conversations made me relaxed. We talked for hours on the telephone.

Why would I travel with someone I didn't know? What if we didn't enjoy each other's company? I used every excuse not to go. This would be the first time I traveled out of the country.

New Year's Day was now upon me and a decision would have to be made soon. A deposit was due to reserve a seat. One night, while talking to Arlene, she said the tour guide was Charlie Toye out of Reading, and Father Joe Whalen would be our spiritual guide.

I was stunned after realizing that these were the two people in my video. *What were the chances of this happening? Was this a sign from God to go?*

I had to let go of the fear that was overtaking me and let Arlene know my decision on the trip. Trying to make a decision to go on this trip made my heart beat like crazy.

The next time Arlene called, I explained my history of palpations, my fear of having problems with my fibrillation and with being away from my cardiologist in a strange country. She was very understanding and told me that one of her sisters had the same heart problem. We discussed the different medicines and techniques her sister used to combat her problem. Nothing seemed to shake Arlene. She never pushed me or got upset when I changed my mind which I did constantly.

The next day, I spent my lunch hour away from work and went to the Taunton Post Office to get my first passport—just in case I wanted to go. I had the necessary pictures taken at the AAA office in Raynham the week before, so I took them with me. I started the ball rolling for the trip but was still not sure about signing up. I pushed the idea of flying to the back of my mind. If I didn't think about it, I wouldn't have to deal with it.

Everyone at the office was happy for me, yet shocked I was going to a war-zone for my vacation. After all, the co-worker who was in the National Guard had no choice, but I did. The topic came up every day at work and I was surprised my fellow workers weren't sick of hearing me talk about Medjugorje. In fact, the conversation did the opposite. My friends were thrilled that I was sharing the details of this event with them.

When they saw I was serious about the trip, they were eager for me to go. My friends took turns bringing my Medjugorje video home to see what was going on in this village and to learn about the apparitions. A large group of employees were involved in my plans for the journey, whether they were Catholic or not.

When the itinerary arrived, I made copies to pass out to the individuals at work. People posted my itinerary on their bulletin boards so they could follow my daily activities when the time came. They wanted to share the whole trip with me from beginning to end.

I volunteered to take petitions from any co-worker, who wanted their written prayers prayed over, by a priest, or a visionary in Medjugorje. They would be presented to Our Lady for Her to answer their requests. I guaranteed each person that the envelopes wouldn't be opened. Debbi Bettencourt, our Human Resource Administrator, was back within the half-hour and placed hers on my desk. I collected forty-two petitions to take with me.

Roadblocks

Testing my faith—but mostly my desire—to go to Medjugorje, roadblocks were about to hit me the likes of which no one would ever have imagined. Poor Charlie, our tour guide, didn't know what I was going to do. First I was going, and then days later, he would get a call from me saying I couldn't bring myself to fly.

Charlie took the time to explain we would be flying on an airbus out of Logan Airport in Boston. He had been on seven trips to Medjugorje on that type of plane and assured me they were the smoothest flights he had ever taken. Charlie warned me not to take the flight out of TF Green Airport in Providence, Rhode Island to Newark, New Jersey. I would be flying on a small prop plane and the flight could be very rough. He advised me to meet the group in Boston.

Finally, embarrassed by my delay in answering, I told Charlie to book me and sent him my deposit. Money was tight, but a miracle happened. I had played my daily number for fifty cents and won $2,000 out of the full $4,000 jackpot. It paid for my whole trip. Our Lady really wanted me there.

About four months before the trip, my doctor scheduled me for a colonoscopy test. I had finished the final preparations for the morning procedure and started to relax in our bedroom for the night. Al was downstairs watching television around 9 p.m. My stomach was growling from hunger and I wanted to go to sleep to make the morning come faster. I couldn't wait to eat a full meal the next day.

When my eyes started to get heavy, I leaned over on my left side and stretched my right hand to switch off the light on the nightstand. Suddenly, my heart started to thump hard with a severely, irregular heartbeat.

My heart bounced like a Ping-Pong ball, going in every direction at a tremendous, high-rate of speed. I tried not to panic. For years, I had fought fibrillation but this was extremely different. It terrified me. There was no pain but breathing was difficult.

I got myself up into a sitting position and sat with my legs dangling over the bed. Most of the time, changing positions during a palpitation episode would help my heart go back into a normal rhythm. This action wasn't working. I got out of bed, held my hand over my heart and took slow, short steps to reach the top of the stairs. Any excursion during these attacks only made my heart race faster. I called out to Al and immediately he knew by the tone of my voice that there was something seriously wrong.

Once Al reached the stairway and saw me at the top having trouble breathing, he came up to check me. He tried to calm me and could see I was short of breath and pale. He had helped me through many attacks, but he started to worry when this one didn't subside.

I grabbed one of my tranquilizers prescribed for this problem. My cardiologist was in Taunton, forty minutes away and with any heart problem, I knew an ambulance would take me to the nearest hospital, which would be Tobey Hospital in Wareham. That meant I would have a different doctor.

I waited a little longer, hoping my heart would get back into a normal rhythm. After a few minutes, I realized this could be serious. I told Al to call the ambulance. This was something I had never had to do. My fibrillation could ordinarily be controlled but not this time. Al feared leaving me to make the call but I told him I'd be okay. I sat again on the edge of the bed, holding my chest and tried to fill my lungs with air. My breathing was shallow and my heart still raced out of control.

The ambulance station was only a few blocks away, so the rescue crew was at our door in minutes. One of the three EMT's ran up to my bedroom. He sat on the edge of the bed next to me and fitted an oxygen mask over my face, while taking my vitals. The other two EMT's came up the steep stairs with a special seat to transport me back down to a stretcher at the bottom of the landing.

One of them told Al, "This kind of problem frequently happens when a person is relaxed in bed for the night."

I felt my heart slow down and return to normal once the oxygen was administered to me and the tranquilizer kicked in. EMT's don't have the authority to determine how serious a person's situation is, so they had to follow through and take me straight to the hospital. Upon my arrival, Dr. Morrow, the doctor on call, examined me. He made the decision to keep me overnight to make sure they weren't missing anything serious, which is normal with a heart patient.

While I was waiting in the hallway to get a room, the doctor came back to see me. He asked if I had other symptoms that bothered me. I informed him I had been experiencing pain between my shoulders blades for a few weeks and asked if the signs could be a gallbladder problem,

He said this discomfort had nothing to do with the heart problem and that it would go away. He wasn't a cardiologist but he set a follow-up appointment for me to see him when I got out of the hospital. Once I started to feel better, I regretted calling the ambulance. Through the years, I handled my smaller episodes by resting and waiting for them to disappear. This was the first time being hospitalized from them. My procedure that had been scheduled the next morning at the hospital was canceled.

The admitting doctor scheduled a cardiologist to see me the next day. My overnight stay became a week. The heart doctor ordered a stress test even though my symptoms didn't return. When the results came back showing no serious heart problems, he talked to me and Al before letting me go home.

The cardiologist decided to take me off my heart pills, claiming he didn't think they were necessary. I had been taking them for over ten years. Stopping them started my fibrillation up again which continued every day for a week. I decided on my own to go back on them after notifying my primary cardiologist. It took five days for the pills to get back into my system and relieve the problem.

After having such a serious fibrillation attack, I started to think twice about going on my trip to Medjugorje. It was coming up soon and my fears about going were stronger than ever.

What would I do in a foreign country, an hour away from the nearest hospital? What if the doctors don't understand English and I went into fibrillation again?

By this time, I was a complete wreck. I was sorry I had agreed to the foolish trip.

I called Charlie and told him about my hospital stay and about how once again, I was having doubts about going.

He tried not to show his frustration and said, "Alberta, a solid decision has to be made within two days, especially with eight people waiting to go if you canceled. Once I fill your spot, you can't retract your decision."

Charlie added to my fear of flying by casually mentioning the trip would involve three flight changes to get there. My heart sank and my knees grew weak just talking to him about this, and I hadn't even left yet.

I thought if Al would come with me, my fears would be gone. *How could I be so insecure on my own?* I was really questioning why I ever agreed to go. I was giving up a vacation to Hawaii with Al to travel to a war zone with someone I didn't even know.

Whatever possessed me to decide something so far out of character for me?

I kept my scheduled appointment with Dr. Morrow, even though I had no idea why I was returning to him since he wasn't a heart doctor.

"How are you feeling?"

"I still have the pain between my shoulder blades and the indigestion in my chest."

He looked irritated, "You're fine."

The doctor was treating me like a neurotic. I didn't need any further problems before my trip, so I decided to let the discomfort go. Maybe subconsciously, I was wishing for things to go wrong so the trip could be called off.

I told Al that night I was thinking about not going.

He looked up from his newspaper, completely surprised, "Really. Why? I thought you wanted to go."

With the way he asked the question and looked so disappointed in me, I realized that backing out would be a mistake. This was the first time in months I had felt Al really wanted me to go. He never talked about my journey. I had many reasons to go and one was to fill Dad's wish of going himself before he died.

Arlene must have been sent from heaven because she always seemed to call when I was in a crisis with my decision to go or not. I explained about going to the hospital and what had happened.

She said, "You do realize that this is the devil working on you? It's normal to hear about people with serious health problems before a pilgrimage. Satan's testing you and your problems are his way of stopping you from completing the trip."

One morning, I was in bed sick, and Al went to the gym. I was totally overcome by changing my mind every other day. The insecure feeling actually had made me sick inside. The fibrillation occurrence had just doubled my fear of getting these attacks while I was in Bosnia.

I got on my knees on top of my bed, with my hands up to God and prayed as hard as anyone could.

My frustration had me actually screaming out loud, "Please, God, help me with this. I can't handle this decision. If it's the devil working on me, let me defeat him."

I asked St. Michael to drive Satan away and get my mind healthy for this trip. I prayed to St. Raphael for healing of my heart problems and asked for peace with my decision. I wanted to stick with going and give it up to God. I actually broke down and cried from the feeling of being lost and weak because of a decision to go somewhere.

Why can't I back out? No one was making me go.

Meanwhile, all my friends at work were excited waiting for me to leave on this trip. Each day my office was filled with people chatting with me about what I was going to experience. There was so much faith restored in some employees and I knew they would lose their belief if I didn't complete the journey. All my talk about God, Our Lady, miracles, and a little town in Bosnia would be lost forever for them.

Maryanne Stevens, who was in customer service, gave me a petition from a friend of hers. The friend's son, Shawn, was in his early twenties and had brain cancer. He was dying and the doctors said he would probably not live another month. His mother put a lock of Shawn's hair in an envelope. Friends with cancer were hanging onto the hope their petitions would be blessed with a cure. People who wished to travel there themselves were living their dreams in my future experiences.

I knew something, or someone, was pulling me to Medjugorje. This wasn't my decision. All I knew was this had to happen—even though I didn't know why.

Arlene called and explained Our Lady calls each individual herself to this location. "If you don't go, Our Lady will be disappointed."

This made me understand why the desire to go was so strong inside of me: I was being called.

There were only four weeks before the trip and I had a doctor's appointment with my cardiologist. We discussed what he believed caused me to be rushed by ambulance to the emergency room. He felt an empty stomach preparing for the colonoscopy made it harder for my heart pills to be absorbed, causing them to offset my heart rhythm. He told me to push my fears aside and not to stop myself from living because of one bad encounter.

"If another attack comes, lie down somewhere and take a pill," he advised. "If the fibrillation doesn't go away in an hour, take another pill and just rest. Don't get overtired because this may make your heart race."

With the doctor's appointments behind me, I put everything in God's hands to get me there. My comfort with the decision had one more test. The pain I complained about between my shoulder blades? It got worse. Here it was three weeks before the trip and poor Al was taking me to another specialist to get the problem checked. The surgeon confirmed my gallbladder had to be removed right away.

"We'll do the surgery next Wednesday."

"That soon?" I said with shock.

"Do you want to be in good health for your trip? The recovery time will only be two weeks. I'll schedule the pre-op testing tomorrow and perform the surgery in two days."

I had no time to really think about the procedure.

The doctor saw the fear on my face and asked, "Do you want to have a serious gallbladder attack when you get there? Get this over with so you can go with no worries."

The surgery was completed with no complications, and I had two weeks to heal completely. Our Lady was knocking hard on my door to get me to Medjugorje! The only thing I didn't question by now was the fact I *had* to go. I knew deep down that if this trip wasn't taken, I'd never go. Once I faced my fear head on, the terror wasn't so intense.

Reunion

May 25, 1998 arrived, three days before my trip, and my excitement was building, to my astonishment. The night before, Al surprised me by making a fabulous lobster dinner for the two of us. A chef would have had a challenge beating Al's homemade scallop dressing. Candles on the table and a bottle of wine added to the exceptional meal. The thoughtfulness was such a special and loving thing for him to do for me before I left. He wasn't one for romantic words but his actions always expressed his emotions.

Once I was on my way, the moment was a combination of anticipation and nervousness. I wished Arlene had met me at Logan Airport in Boston, but living in West Warwick, Rhode Island, it only made sense for her to fly from T.F. Green Airport in Providence. She was boarding a prop plane to meet the group in New Jersey. The jet sounded much better to me. As much as I feared flying, I wanted to hear and feel the power of a jet engine under me, when we took off.

The idea of leaving Leona behind was heartbreaking. She claimed the lumberyard was too busy for her to take a week off. She never flew and I think she feared the flight worse than me, if that was possible. She swore to never fly. I had strong feelings she couldn't overcome the fright and that was the real reason she stayed home. Her panic was something I could understand. We both had planned and prayed to share this trip together. Before I left, she gave me her rosary beads and Dad's cross pendant to take for a blessing in Medjugorje.

Al drove me to Logan Airport in Boston. I had hoped someone in my area was going on the same trip so we could

142

have shared in the expense of a van and save Al the hour long trip. I still wished he was coming with me but finally accepted the fact that this journey was meant to be mine, not his.

We arrived at 11a.m. at the airport and Al parked the car in front of the terminal to check in my luggage. My only wish now was to find the tour group. I longed to see Charlie or Father Whalen. I had no idea where to go in the airport and followed behind Al like a lost puppy. No matter what direction he took, he had me on his heels. Al had always made the decisions about traveling so I depended on him to get me to the right gate for my flight. It had never crossed my mind that someday I might travel without him.

Charlie Toye had mailed a package out to everyone on his tour. It contained a red baseball cap to wear so we would all be identified as Charlie's Angels from The Spirit of Medjugorje Tours. No one from the group was waiting in sight when we reached the gate. I was trying not to push the anxiety button inside me. Since Al left the car unattended, he couldn't stay with me too long. I tried to hide my shaking from him. Al waited ten minutes to see if someone from the tour group would show up. If I saw one person from the gang, I would have been put at ease.

Finally Al had no choice but to go back to the car. He gave me a hug before departing and I smiled, waving like a frequent traveler before he turned the corner. While my insides were in knots, I faked being at ease. I honestly wanted to grab onto my husband's ankle when he turned to leave. This was either going to make or break me with traveling alone.

It was twenty minutes before the scheduled flight was due to leave and I was still standing alone. *Where's the group? Please, God, I'm scared enough.* Countless times I checked my ticket to see if I was at the correct gate and airline. If I wasn't, I would have been in tears not knowing what to do or where to go. Except for one woman sitting in a corner, the gate area was completely empty. I couldn't believe a flight was ready to leave with no people waiting to board. *I have to be in the wrong place,* I thought.

Having time on my hands started me thinking nothing but negative thoughts. *Maybe I'm nuts traveling to a country with a war going on. What if our flight hit severe turbulence or worse, crashed?* I went up to a sales counter to get a magazine to read and purchased hard candies in case my ears popped during the flight. I had to keep moving. The more I pictured myself going on the plane, the sicker I became.

Ten minutes before boarding, a group of fifteen to twenty people walked up to the gate. They all had red hats! What a tremendous relief, seeing Father Whalen and Charlie Toye. I recognized them from my video at home. I went over to Charlie and introduced myself. I thought he might not be excited meeting the insane woman he had been speaking to for the past five months. To make my first impression with him worse, he told me they had been waiting at the baggage area for *me* to arrive. I had over-looked the itinerary page that stated where to meet.

It was now 2 p.m. and we were called to board our plane. Although my legs felt like they didn't belong to me, they were moving and holding me up. My heart was racing. On the outside, I looked calm, but I felt like a five-year-old in a strange place....left alone! I imagined my legs straight as boards and someone pushing me from behind to get me on the airplane. *How can a person have so much paralyzing fear?* I didn't want an attack of fibrillation from anxiety. I prayed over and over again, to help me stay relaxed.

The group was divided and sat in different sections of the plane. Not one person on the tour was near me. I noted where everyone sat so that when they got off the plane, I would see what direction they headed next. I sat myself at the assigned window seat, when a young girl, looking to be in her late twenties, sat next to me. She casually admitted that she had fear of flying. I knew she wasn't going to be giving me any support with *my* anxiety. We spoke to compose ourselves from nerves.

The take-off was smooth. As we ascended, I held my breath and dug my fingers into the armrest until we leveled off. The weather couldn't have been more beautiful. There wasn't a cloud in the sky and the sun was shining. The Lord gave me my first gift. To my amazement, a combination of excitement and peace came over me. As I looked out the window, I mentally spoke to Our Lady.

I'm coming home to you. I stepped over the devil and beat all the roadblocks with heart problems, surgery and terror.

The plane hit some small turbulence, but I remembered what my friend, Heidi, from work said to do when it happened.

"If there's turbulence, close your eyes and pretend you're in a car on a bumpy road."

Believe it or not, the idea worked. If anyone watched me, they would have wondered why I was smiling from ear to ear. I was so proud of myself. Nothing else mattered in my life at this moment, not even my family. This was the first time I was doing something *by* myself and *for* myself. Of course, I almost had a breakdown, but I was here. The flight was going to last forty-five minutes. I sat back and looked out the window and wondered what I was going to experience on this pilgrimage.

We landed at 3p.m. in Newark. I ran to keep up with the group and blended right in with them. Independence was trying hard to kick in. I looked at my tickets and tried to learn gate and flight numbers. The first thing I wanted to do was to spot Arlene so I would see a familiar face. This would be the first time seeing her after our one meeting seven months ago at LaSalette Shrine.

On our way to the boarding gate, I finally noticed her. She laughed seeing my new short, boyish haircut since I never told her about it. We all headed for the assigned gate for our next flight to Prague, and Arlene began describing the flight on the prop plane and how bumpy the trip was the whole time.

"Lucky you didn't take off from Providence."

She was right about being lucky; I would have had knees like jelly getting on the next plane.

I watched everyone in our party mixing together from all different states. Some people mingled and talked with former friends they had connected to on other pilgrimages.

I listened and watched closely as individuals grouped together and spoke about being on their fourth or seventh trip to Medjugorje. I was shocked and wondered how anyone wanted to do the same thing every year. People who landed from other flights ran up and hugged each other renewing friendships from shared pilgrimages in the past. I felt like a newborn to a spiritual world.

Wouldn't they want to have some fun at a vacation spot sometime? After all, how many religious trips could they take without being bored?

I couldn't imagine leaving Al home every year while I went on trips alone.

Arlene introduced me to a very good friend of hers from Warwick, Rhode Island. His name was Eddie Sousa and his son, Ed, Jr., was with him. Ed, Jr. was studying to become a priest and this was also his first trip to Medjugorje. Little did I know the tight bond that we would all develop from this journey.

I would soon learn how my spiritual renewals would be reborn. I couldn't wait to deliver all the petitions from family and friends and to make the trip for my father.

Before boarding the plane at 5:30 p.m., Father Joe blessed individuals with holy water and prayed for a safe trip. Passengers not on the tour watched us with inquisitive looks.

We entered the airbus, which held over four hundred passengers. Arlene and I shared two seats together by a window. I was happy with the seating arrangement because I never liked being squished in the long middle row with an outsider.

We were locked in together for a full eight hours while flying to Prague. To my complete astonishment, there wasn't any uneasiness with Arlene or me. The only thing we found missing was time to catch our breath from talking non-stop which has never changed through the years.

As the hours passed, we learned about one another's likes and dislikes. Our Lady certainly knew who to pick to transport me to Medjugorje.

Arlene and I talked about everything from our childhood years right up to the present moment. Her last name was Albert, and I had a twin brother, Albert. We both had sisters named Leona. One sister had heart problems, like me, and we both had a brother who died. There were six children in my family and Arlene had fourteen. Our interests blended together, but the most important conversations consisted of Medjugorje. She couldn't tell me enough about this village.

It was eleven o'clock in the evening and we decided to try to get some rest. I leaned my head back and I remembered the doctor had advised me not to get overtired. Knowing that we would be in Medjugorje the next day brought my anticipation higher and it was hard to fall asleep.

When midnight arrived, we passed through the time change and the dark evening sky was changed into a beautiful sunrise. I never had this experience while traveling. The blinding sun's reflection off the plane's wing hurt my eyes and I turned away. Arlene stared directly into the brightness smiling with contentment. She never blinked once. Eddie walked down the aisle, leaned over me to look out our widow and asked Arlene if she saw the miracle of the sun. Arlene described the sun spinning with soft shades of pink, blue, purple and gold. She said when the colors encircled the sun, it pulsated.

"Can you see it?" she asked me.

The blazing sun was so powerful that I couldn't imagine how either of them could look directly into the heavenly body. I took fast, short glances and my eyes watered. I feared they could be damaged by staring at something so intense. I sat back letting the two of them enjoy their miracle. I knew in time, Our Lady would show me if that was Her wish.

Prague to Medjugorje

We landed in Prague at 7:45 a.m. Charlie was right about the smooth ride of the airbus. It had been like sitting in a living room. Leona would have had a great experience for her first time flying.

We came off the plane exhausted from the long eight hours of air travel. We carried small overnight bags for our stay in Prague. Our luggage was transported to another plane for the next day's flight. What a relief that we didn't have to drag our baggage anywhere when we were so tired.

We boarded the bus that traveled outside the city area. The back roads passed private properties that displayed unkempt yards with trash bags and broken down cars. The traffic was fast and busy at intersections. Within a half hour we reached the Kladno Hotel. The lodging had a strange appearance because it was built not only tall, but very narrow. Charlie had told us that the hotels in Europe were not going to have the comfort we have in the United States.

The hotel hallway at the check-in counter was in good shape. The restaurant to our left looked clean with fresh flowers on the tables. The elevator was old and only carried two people. During the war, the lift was used to carry only food carts. The hotel management never replaced the old hoist with a new modern one. Although Arlene and I felt squished inside, I enjoyed the experience when we rode on it. At this point, all I wanted was an elevator to get me to my room with a bed and shower.

Charlie gave everyone two hours to wash and get refreshed before lunch and a city tour. We left the Newark International

148

Airport at 5 p.m. and arrived in Prague at 8 a.m. their time, which was over fourteen hours after leaving my house for Logan Airport. My body felt like it weighed a ton. *Please God, don't let me get my fibrillation.*

Arlene and I tried to rest for an hour but not even a snooze was possible. I felt weak and nauseated from lack of sleep. We both decided to get up, take a shower and go meet the others. The cool water pouring down on my body gave me more energy. The restaurant was small with beautiful scenic paintings of the city buildings and countryside. Tall, colorful, potted flowers were in vases along the walls. The eating time was loud with everyone trying to talk at once about the flight and the anticipation of what awaited us with our tour through Prague. I was surprised that nineteen people on our pilgrimage were by themselves, leaving only seven couples.

After lunch, the bus was parked out front and waited for the group. I tried to push my fatigue aside to enjoy my trip. All of us were dropped off at a corner two blocks from the busy city and told to meet there at 7 p.m. Everyone had a choice to join Charlie and Father Whalen or go on their own. Arlene and I went with the tour group.

The artwork on the buildings was breathtaking. I read once that Prague was one of the most beautiful cities in the world and the sights proved the statement. Keeping the original buildings in Europe has been a practice since ancient times everywhere and not so much in the United States. The older they were, the more splendid they seemed to me. I loved the cobblestone streets.

Charlie pointed out the important sights and talked about their history as we walked through the city.

Father Whalen scheduled a Mass at 2:30 p.m. at Our Lady of Victory Church. The cathedral is of quite exceptional significance, not only because of its architecture and artistic decoration, but in particular because it preserved and venerated the famous statue of the Infant Jesus of Prague.

The Infant of Prague is a devotion to the Infant Christ, a Christian devotion encouraged by the gospel stories of Jesus' birth, and it took a special form in the 17th century when a statue of the Christ Child became the object of honor in the city of Prague, Czechoslovakia. The Infant, holding a globe of the world in His left hand and His right hand extended in blessing, was enthroned in the Church of Our Lady of Victories in 1628. From there, devotion to the Infant of Prague spread throughout the Christian world. Honoring the Infant we honor the "wonder of the Incarnation." Jesus Christ, a tiny Child dwelling among his people, fulfills God's promise to dwell with us simply and familiarly, and blesses our world as well as the humble circumstances of individual lives.

O INFANT JESUS,
Have Mercy on Us!

When Charlie opened the church door, all I saw was gold throughout the whole chapel. There was so much gold in the statues, lights, and the décor that the site caused me to just stand there in wide-eyed wonderment. A side door led to a gift store where I purchased the Prague and Holy Spirit medals to save especially for the men back home. I hoped that fifteen would be enough.

I walked into the church and went up to the altar to see the Infant Jesus of Prague. The gold sculpture was hidden in the floor to ceiling gold alter. I kneeled and prayed in front of this famous statue of Jesus. So much history resonated all around me.

First prayers centered on Shawn, a boy I had never met who was fighting for his life with cancer and his presence was deep in my soul. He was due to pass away before my return. I prayed for God to give him more time. I held the envelope that contained the locket of Shawn's hair along with all the petitions and rosary beads. I laid every item down at the altar rail. I prayed for each individual who needed healing.

Father Whalen called us to sit in the pews while he started a Mass in this holy church. I held my friend Rita's rosary in my hand as Mass was being said. I took turns holding different rosaries given to me including my father's. Father Whalen prayed over all the letters we had brought from home and blessed them through the Holy Spirit. When he mentioned praying for the people who couldn't come, I thought of Leona. She would have loved witnessing all this with me. I told her before leaving that the Blessed Mother must not have been calling her at this time. With all my roadblocks before leaving on this trip, I knew that nothing on Earth will get in one's way if she is calling you.

After leaving the church, the group walked to a long, stone bridge. Along its length artists painted and sold their pictures. Tourists sat in chairs and had their portraits done. I felt a peaceful joy as I watched the artists painting. The European buildings and churches behind the bridge gave me a deeper appreciation for the talent behind their master drawings on canvas. I was disappointed when we moved on to another location.

During our walk we saw old churches, quaint little restaurants and wonderful statues in and outside of every building. Except for attending Mass, we walked from 1 p.m. to 7 p.m. without resting. By now, I had severe pain in my legs and hips. I didn't know if I could make it to the bus. What a

151

welcome sight to see the motor vehicle waiting for us at the corner.

The transport dropped us back at the hotel where we were served a late supper. Arlene and I couldn't wait to go straight to bed. My mind was in a daze and my body begged for sleep. There was little conversation that night and sleep was thankfully not a problem.

The next morning, we were up at 5 a.m. to get the 7:20 a.m. flight to Zagreb, the capital of Bosnia. What a difference in alertness, after getting a full night's sleep. My rest was going to make it easier to face another full day of activities.

At the airport, I expected to see a jet and instead, we walked on the runway to a prop plane. The flight was a little bumpy, but to avoid being on edge, I concentrated only on the enthusiasm of knowing today we would be in Medjugorje.

When we landed in Zagreb, we had our last connection to the city of Split. The airport in Split was very small. Handlers brought our luggage to us without any waiting and went out the front doors to board the motor coach. About ten buses were lined up in the parking lot waiting to take the tourists on their three hour ride to Medjugorje.

Arlene was excited to be back for the second time. She tried to remember which side of bus she sat on last time to view the Adriatic Sea. She said the scenery was spectacular and wanted me to see the area. Here was a poor country, destroyed by a war, and Our Lady chose to appear in this devastated land.

It was summertime during our visit. Cattle and sheep roamed the open fields and gave me a feeling of stillness.

Children stood by the roadside, waving and smiling as the buses passed. They wore clothes that were very simple and plain. At home my clothes were packed so tightly together in my closet that I had trouble pulling them out. *Why do we need so much?*

I thought about how much the trip cost and that families here had probably never left their country. In their lifetimes they might have never seen the other side of the world, but will be happy knowing God gave them so much. I believed their pleasures came from their family life, tending the animals, and working in the fields together. As we cruised along the dirt roads, I wondered how many people standing along the roadside had lost family members because of the war. I would have been gratified to talk to the residents and listen to their stories.

The bus driver pulled over to the right side of the road when he came to a small, unmarked cemetery. If he hadn't pointed out this location, it could have been easily missed with no signs. He told us that only soldiers from the war were buried there. The graveyard looked to have had only twenty caskets encased above the ground. After a few minutes, the bus moved slowly from the burial ground. I glanced fast and saw the names of the soldiers and the dates of their passing were written on the top of the coffin enclosed in cement.

Halfway to Medjugorje we stopped at a replica shrine of Our Lady of Lourdes, built by the bishop of Split after he visited the original at Lourdes, France. He realized that he had in his diocese an exact replica of the cave in France. A small mountain site was dug out to fit a statue of Our Lady, an altar and a black, iron stand that would hold about a hundred candles for the pilgrims to light. The statue of the Blessed Mother had a white dress with a white, full-length veil edged with gold. She had a wide, blue, flowing belt that went around Her waist that fell halfway down the front of Her dress, which was also edged in gold. Above Her head was a gold circular ring that had JA SAM NEOSKVRN JENO ZACCE written on it. Gold, pink, red and white roses were placed at the bottom of Her feet and on both sides of the statue. Groups of candles were lit throughout the cave with other religious statues of St. Francis, Jesus and St. Joseph.

This shrine was an active healing site with the same spiritual and healing charismas as the original. At least forty benches outside faced the grotto where people sat and prayed. A large group of thirty nuns walked around the grounds. Charlie told us that the sisters lived at the monastery right up the hill and came down to give thanks here daily.

Father Whalen prepared to say Mass outside at the grotto. I was sure celebrating Mass in the open air would be refreshing. Anyone in the shrine area had been welcomed to join in the service. Fr. Whalen blessed everyone and started the Mass. Father appointed a few from our group to help with the readings. When the ceremony was completed, we made a short visit to a tiny gift store.

Inspired, everyone boarded the bus and settled into their assigned seats. Father Whalen led us through one decade of the rosary and everyone's voices blended in with the prayer. If I hadn't learned the rosary during Dad's illness, I wouldn't have had the understanding of how to say the prayer and what it was about. When we finished praying, I looked out of the window to take in the majestic mountains. Trees lined the lower cliffs and the rest of the higher mounts had rock formations. Stone houses and businesses were all built at the bottom of the mountains and along the Adriatic Sea. Small villages were constructed in the valleys with the high peaks of mountaintops that surrounded them.

Arlene leaned over with a warm smile and whispered, "So, how do you feel, being in Medjugorje?"

My emotions were overwhelming and tears started down my checks. I looked back out the window to keep from breaking down completely. Arlene saw me fighting for control and didn't press me to talk.

How was I so blessed to be chosen to come here? I thought trying to understand my own miracles which will come from the apparitions.

Travel Map from Zagreb to Medjugorje

The main road map of Bosnia and Herzegovina

The Village of Medjugorje

I was awakened from my unconsciousness of daydreaming on top of Apparition Hill as I heard Arlene's voice. It brought me back to our climb that we had just completed.

"Hey, I've been looking for you. The group is starting to depart from the mountain and go back to the house," Arlene said, as she sat down on the grass next to me.

"I was sitting here soaking up the sun, and was studying how beautiful the village of Medjugorje is from this height. I had so much peace, and the sun felt so warm on me, I must have fallen asleep. I started thinking back about how I came on this pilgrimage and our meeting. I'm glad we met at LaSalette. What a miracle."

"That wasn't a miracle, Alberta. Our Lady had that happen. Every person who comes here is because She calls them. She put us together."

"You're right. Look. You can see the steeple of St. James Church standing high above everything in the village," I said pointing toward the tower.

"The church is the center of everything here."

Arlene and I talked about our spiritual feelings before leaving. What a renewal this was for me.

After an hour, we started to slowly descend from the hill. At the bottom was a small, enclosed booth where a vendor sold food and drinks. Both of us ordered a cold beverage to refresh ourselves. The young girl serving us said the weather was extremely hot for this time of year. The temperature was already in the nineties. Little did we know the climate was going to get even hotter.

On our way back to the house, we passed through some gift stores in the village. I caught sight of an outstanding statue of the Blessed Mother. All the facial details were not only softly colored but sharp. Her eyes penetrated mine and Her smile was defined. Our Lady's gown and veil were light gray like the visionaries described Her. The sculpture showed Her beauty.

"Arlene, I'd love to see how much a statue like this would cost to ship home." This figure was so different from the ones I'd find at home."

"Wait. I have a strong feeling that Al's going to buy you one while you're here."

Laughing under my breath I remarked, "Al....buying me a statue? I don't think so, Arlene!"

I spoke of Al's absence from church, but her remark made me hold off in case a miracle did happen.

We spent little time shopping due to the heat and the fact that we had to walk to the other side of the village to get to our house. We enjoyed our return, traveling toward the open fields. On our way, Arlene and I wandered through a back trail. We came upon a family dwelling that was constructed right at the edge of the path. The living quarter was a hut with gaps between the sideboards, which allowed us to see right through the home. I couldn't help but wonder what the family did in the cold winter months.

Behind the house was a fallen down barn-like structure. The shack was low and rickety, with a crumpling roof. Three sides of the building were barely standing and leaned halfway to the ground. One side had already collapsed and gave little shelter for the animals. The animals gave off an extremely foul and unpleasant odor. The sun hit their stables and the heat intensified their stench. I held my breath as we passed by. We were careful to avoid stepping in the animal waste.

An elderly man and his wife fed their goats and they seemed to own nothing more than the two worn-out buildings and the animals. The path in front of their property was dry, cracked mud.

The couple gazed at the both of us with warm smiles as we passed by. They probably wondered about us the same as we did about them. I thought of how many pilgrims must pass in front of their property day after day, yet they showed no signs of being annoyed. At that moment, I longed to speak their language so I could learn about their lives and understand their culture.

The hot air didn't give us any relief when we reached the open fields. The full sun beat down on us. It drained the little energy I had left from the day. The soft wind made the tall blades of grass in the fields sway slowly. The snapping sounds of June bugs could be heard but not seen.

Along the path, vendors had tents set up to protect them from the scalding sun while they sold their homemade, colorful blankets and holy items. We bought rosaries because the prices were cheaper than at the stores in the center of town.

Arlene and I came upon an immense field bursting with red, poppy flowers. There were African American men and women standing among the overflowing, scarlet blossoms taking pictures. Arlene asked if they wanted her to take their pictures surrounded by the perennials then they could do the same for us.

They spoke French and Arlene impressed me when she spoke the language fluently. I knew she was born in Canada but didn't know she was French and spoke the dialect. We took turns snapping pictures and then continued toward our village.

It wasn't long before we came upon a shaded but thickly wooded area. I couldn't get over the number of birds singing in the trees. No matter where we traveled, the noise from the flocking feathered friends was overpowering. We were surrounded by them. Their chirps were enjoyable to listen to because I've always felt flowers and birds were the most beautiful things God had created.

When we reached the village, people wandered through the small marketplace looking for the best deals. On Sundays, the devout Catholic vendors closed their gift stands. They give up profits to spend the day worshipping.

Arlene and I wanted to rest our feet after walking all morning. We went to the benches to pray by the statue of Our Lady in front of St. James Church. I became aware that Arlene was looking directly at the sun wearing her sunglasses. She asked if I wanted to see the miracle of the sun. I could tell she desperately wanted me to share in her gift.

Each time I looked up, the sun was still blinding. It was impossible for me.

I repeated, "If Our Lady wants me to see it, she'll show me."

I didn't want to seek out occurrences that happened to others. I took comfort in knowing that if it was meant to be, miracles would be placed in my path.

Eddie Sousa spotted us and came to join in our conversation. I hadn't seen him since the bus had dropped us off at the house. He and his son, Ed Jr., had gone in a different direction with another group. Eddie senior was his late fifties, 5'5" with black hair with black-rimmed glasses. His son was the picture of his father with the same black hair and same height. Both of them were always smiling.

This was the second trip to Medjugorje for both of them. I would be leaving at the end of the week, and they had made arrangements with Arlene to stay another week. They were retired and had the time. I tried not to think of returning and leaving them behind.

Eddie startled me with an unexpected question. "Well, Alberta, how does it feel to be at Medjugorje?"

My emotions surfaced again, and I broke down in loud, long sobs. I couldn't control myself.

He sat next to me and put his arm around my shoulder. "It's very emotional, isn't it? I did the same thing the first three days when I arrived here last year."

Eddie told me about his years as a police officer for the West Warwick Police Department in Rhode Island. Back then, he had no interest in the spiritual world. He explained how his wife, Donna, had been to Medjugorje a few times and kept asking him to go with her. He didn't mind her taking the trips, but he had absolutely no desire to go. It reminded me of Al's way of thinking. For some unknown reason, Eddie suddenly had no other longing but to come to Medjugorje. Like all who are called, he read everything about the village and the apparitions. Now, here he was on his second pilgrimage, with his son.

Ed Jr. was studying to become a priest but struggled with his doubts about whether or not this was really his mission. He was told by others to visit Patrick and Nancy Latta when he came to Medjugorje. Nancy was an interpreter for Father Jozo and had helped many priests with their vocation. Ed, Jr. was now praying for some sign to help him make a decision to enter the priesthood.

Tents along the path selling religious items

Cross Mountain in the background

Tours and Sites in Medjugorje

Charlie had scheduled the group to meet another visionary, Ivan Dragicevic. Ivan was going to tell his story in the village park and, like all the visionaries, he would have an interpreter. We arrived at the park around 2 p.m. and a huge crowd had already gathered. The location was shadowed by trees, so the heat was bearable. The temperature was climbing and anything that helped keep us cool was a relief.

Ivan was the oldest of the male visionaries and was born on May 25th, 1965 in Bijakovici. Our Lady had been appearing to him every day since June 24, 1981. His wife, Laureen Murphy, was a former Massachusetts beauty queen and lived in Boston for six months out of the year. He was asked by Our Lady to pray for the young and for priests.

Ivan looked to be about 5' 6" tall with black hair. He had a serious and business-like expression. His clothing consisted of brown dress pants and a white, tan and deep brown striped summer shirt. As soon as he started his interpreter repeated his message. "The apparitions have made a big difference in my life. Now I arrange to make praying time during the day. Before, my life had no meaning. Today, I'm filled with inner contentment. The first time I saw Our Lady, a change occurred in my soul and in my heart. I often avoided prayer, but now the difference is so great I really can't describe it. I'm not sorry Our Lady revealed my future. I'm confident and not afraid, because I know who leads me and therefore, I'm not afraid of death. All people should feel that way."

Someone asked if he was ever aware of people around him when Our Blessed Mother appeared to him.

161

Ivan replied, "I'm in total ecstasy and never aware of anything or anyone around me. My total concentration is only on Our Lady."

Ivan spoke for about a half hour and by then, the heat had become uncomfortable, so he answered a few questions and ended his talk.

Arlene and I went back to sit in front of Our Lady's statue at St. James Church. Arlene was now determined for me to witness the miracle of the sun. She picked up my sunglasses and handed them to me. "Put these on and do what I tell you. Look up at the sun for a second and then look away. Keep doing this until you don't have to turn away from it."

I tried to please her by doing as she instructed. I did this four times. Gradually, each interval didn't seem as intense as the time before. Finally, I could stare right into the sun and not turn away. A host covered the front of the sun except for the circumference. Pilgrims who come to Medjugorje describe the host as the same shape as the one received in Holy Communion during Mass.

The colors of blue, green, purple, red and pink formed around the rim of the sphere. Our Lady had let me see the miracle! Here I was, looking right into it without my eyes watering. *How could this be?* Multiple colors blended together like a rainbow.

At 5 p.m. we started back to the house because supper was ready to be served. The table we chose was next to the kitchen where family members worked together. Each person had certain responsibilities for preparing the meal so that the food would be served all at once, hot and on time. I couldn't imagine cleaning up twice a day after thirty people or more at each sitting.

Pitchers of water and juice were already on the table. The cold juice went down nicely after a day in the hot sun. I'm not normally the type to drink a lot of fluid, but with the intense heat, I craved cold liquids. During the day, many people carried bottled water with them. This was something I didn't do, but probably should have.

After supper, we sat awhile and conversed. Arlene introduced me to a few friends of hers that she had met on her last trip to Medjugorje. Penny Trice came all the way from Denver, Colorado, Elizabeth Crupi was from Scarsdale, New York and Barbara Goodier was from Cumberland, Rhode Island. Instantly, I felt a connection to the stories of how they all came to Medjugorje. I soon discovered why friendships weren't lost after a pilgrimage. From the meeting, Arlene and I traveled to different locations during the week with the other women.

It was a beautiful night, so we decided to go back to St. James Church to sit on the benches. It was nearly 6:30 p.m., ten minutes to the time until Our Lady appeared to the visionaries. She appeared to them, even if they were out of the country. As we waited, birds chirped loudly. I looked up and saw them flying back and forth in every direction around the nests they had built under the eaves of the church. I suddenly remembered that my book had mentioned that the birds stopped all sound and movement when Our Lady appeared. This was an event I wanted to personally witness. As they came and went with food for their babies in their nest, my eyes never left them. There were hundreds of them. I was surprised that none of them collided considering their speed and numbers.

Exactly at 6:40 p.m., the priest's voice went out over the outside speakers telling everyone that Our Lady was appearing. Every Mass stopped at this time. At that precise moment, I watched closely as every activity from the birds stopped. They were nowhere in sight. The apparition lasted around seven minutes. Once the apparition ended, the birds went right back into their routine as though nothing had happened. It was something one had to see with one's own eyes. Even the birds had felt Her presence.

Arlene and I headed back to the house. It was already close to ten o'clock. I was exhausted and went to bed. Arlene extended her evening on the front patio and joined the others who wanted to linger longer outside.

163

The next morning, Arlene informed me that Pat and Nancy Latta had unexpectedly stopped by the house last night to explain to our tour group how they both came to Medjugorje to live. They had talked about how their lives had changed.

I had seen a picture of Patrick Latta in my tapes. He had thin gray hair with wire-framed glasses. In 1991, Patrick, a successful businessman and car dealer in Canada, and his wife Nancy, a commercial lawyer, received a great grace of conversion through the messages of Our Lady of Medjugorje. Nancy had shoulder length blonde hair and a tiny frame. They left behind everything they had created in their material world and they moved to Medjugorje in 1993, during the height of the war. Fr. Slavko Barbaric, OFM was their spiritual guide and confessor.

Left: Eddie Sousa, Sr, Father Ed, Pat and Nancy Latta

The next morning, after Arlene told me their story, she took me to the post office that was situated at the other end of the village away from the shops. Since we had arrived two days ago, I wanted to call Al. This was the only place where public telephones were available for outside calls.

No one seemed to be stirring at 8 a.m. and the early morning walk was enjoyable with cool air, instead of midday heat.

The post office had one room with a lobby containing six telephones on a wall and one person at a window for services. It felt good to hear Al's voice when we were connected. Talking to him brought me right back to my familiar world.

I love my family but already longed to stay here. I had started to feel that this way of life in this little village was how we were intended to live. I dreaded the idea of returning home to my old lifestyle and habits of rushing here and there to accomplish the everyday tasks. I worried that my praying would fade into the background.

I tried to tell Al everything I'd seen and experienced in the past few days. He interrupted to give me some terrible news. My ex-sister-in-law, Anita Lopes, had open-heart surgery which upset her husband, Sonny, so badly that he had a stroke and both were in the same hospital. Sonny was my ex-husband's brother. They owed the Lopes Construction Company in Taunton and both my daughters, Debbie and Lori, worked for their aunt and uncle.

I panicked. Sonny previously had two major heart attacks. Being so far away, I wondered how quickly travel arrangements could be made if anything happened to either of them.

Al sensed the distress in my voice. "Calm down. The best thing you can do is to pray for them to get better while you're there."

I knew he was right. Rosaries were the strongest prayers for the sick. This was a time to turn to my faith. I asked Al to tell the family we'd be praying for them.

Arlene knew by my expression that something dreadful had happened to someone. I gave her the details and she said there was time to catch the 10 a.m. Mass to pray for them.

We headed back and got in the line already forming at the side door of the church. Ahead of me I observed a boy in a wheelchair one of the many disabled who had come to Medjugorje. He looked to be in his early twenties. His warm smile suggested his high spirits. One person, out of many, who was disabled and had come to Medjugorje looking for miracles.

His father was adjusting him in the seat to make him more comfortable.

"What's your son's name?" I asked.

"Frank."

"I'll say a prayer for him in church."

"Thank you."

Strangers were touching my life, leaving me with the desire to help them.

Meanwhile, more people arrived and created a tremendous crowd outside. It was a miracle in itself to see how hundreds of pilgrims could squeeze into this church. As we waited, Arlene took her rosary beads out of the pouch. I noticed that the inside of the white, linen lining had gold that looked like rust spots.

"Arlene, why do you have rust spots in the pouch?"

She rubbed the lining with her thumb, thinking the color would come out.

"Turn the pocket inside out so we can get a better look," I suggested.

Arlene turned the sack and looked at me with a shocked expression.

"Tell me what you see to confirm what's facing me," she said.

There was the clear outline of the Blessed Mother from the waist up, with Her head bent down, covered with Her veil. The image was detailed in two different shades of gold. The outline showed Her holding the baby Jesus. He was leaning His back against Her with His knees bent. The form was stained in the lining. Her rosary chain links were gold.

"Last year, my rosaries turned gold but this stained imprint was not in the lining." Arlene said.

Before she had the chance to put them away, the church doors opened. This time, I knew to move in promptly with everyone else so I could get to an unoccupied pew. Arlene and I were fortunate to find a seat together. As the Mass began, I prayed for Frank, Anita, and Sonny. I learned that both Anita and Sonny had recuperated. *How strong are prayers with faith?*

There were so many men in church who weren't shy about belting out the songs. Their deep voices blended in perfectly with the women's higher-pitched tones. I looked around the church and I couldn't find one person who wasn't singing.

I wondered why people back home treated Mass like it was a chore to attend. On special holy days, like Easter or Christmas, parishioners performed their "yearly duty." Years ago, I was one of them. No one felt they needed God anymore.

It was only an hour a week out of our lives. What were we all doing to our souls?

Confession and Penance

Following the services, Arlene and I found contentment once again just by sitting on the benches outside the church. My concentration this time was on the eight confessional boxes and I noticed the priests were already inside them and the lines were very small. (As of 2011, construction work has begun at the St. James' Church by building 36 new confessionals. The parish of Medjugorje will take the total number to 61, more than doubling today's 25 confessionals.)

I reflected on how I had not been going to confession and still received Holy Communion. I felt ashamed about not going monthly to confession as Our Lady asked. A few of my friends believed we didn't have to go to confession. I felt that when we acknowledge our sins the action made us *aware* of them and we won't keep committing the same sin. I don't understand the thought that the faithful can go straight to God and bypass a priest. Priests give us absolution to cleanse our souls and bring us closer to Our Lord and this helps give us strength to fight the devil. God gave them the right to do this. This is a great gift.

In the Medjugorje books, the visionaries stressed the importance of confession. They were educated about this by Our Lady the first year She appeared to them. During an early apparition, the Blessed Mother started to allow the crowd to feel Her presence. Some claimed they felt heat or a current in the space they were told She was positioned.

After a very short time, She told the visionaries to put an end to individuals touching Her. She explained the people were so full of sin, that they were soiling Her white gown. The

Blessed Mother wanted them to go to confession to cleanse themselves from their sins and to confess as soon as possible.

This information gave me the insight and knowledge about how strong our sins are against God and our own souls. He gives us graces so we can develop the strength to combat Satan. It's easy to not know this when we don't see or feel these gifts. Many need to see to believe.

What has happened to faith? The more we pray from the heart, the more Jesus helps us. The Holy Spirit leads us out of temptation. Leaving God out of our lives, leaves us wide open for Satan to control us.

Our Lady told the visionaries that the number one sin souls commit and cause them to go to Hell is lust. I never would have known that if I had not read the books. This statement from Her is important to think about with our way of living. That's why we have to be prepared and clean from sin when we are called home.

It's written, *"Be sure of this: if the master of the house had known the hour when the thief was coming, he would not have let his house be broken into. You also must be prepared, for at an hour you do not expect, the Son of Man will come." (Luke 12:35-40)*

I decided to get in line and make a good confession. An incident lay heavy on my soul for years even though it had been confessed in the past. I carried guilt when I forced my daughter, Lori, into an abortion when she was seventeen. Being divorced, I tried to handle three jobs to meet my monthly bills. In the eighties, unmarried, pregnant girls were still banished from society. The thought of her going through life with a child alone and a nice boy not wanting to marry her, made this decision important at the time, especially since I stopped being active in the Church. I didn't have God in my soul. I was blinded to the fact that God was giving us a new life in our family. I learned that God had a reason for every child who comes into this world, planned or not. Years didn't erase my action. It still haunts me.

I felt the sin should be confessed again. Since I was in Medjugorje, I felt closer to God. *This is the place for God to really hear me and understand how sorry I am.* As I went into the English confessional box, I prayed God would lead me to the most sympathetic priest. I took my time explaining to Father what was bothering me. He was very compassionate and understanding.

Then I made the worst possible move. My confession was almost completed when I admitted that this had been confessed to another priest years ago, but I still felt guilt. I shared a tiny closure with only a thin drape separating me from the priest. He lost all control and got offended. He replied in such a loud and irritated voice, his power made me jump and removed me from the spell of holiness.

He firmly stated, "Don't ever confess a sin a second time or carry guilt once you are forgiven. When a priest forgives you…God forgives you. If you carry guilt, you're letting the devil win and control your soul by making you feel God doesn't love or isn't compassionate to forgive. If a priest forgives, it's forgotten in God's eyes!"

I never imagined a priest displaying such dissatisfaction with someone in confession.

I told him, "I never thought carrying guilt as the work of the devil."

He then gave me my penance.

I opened the small door and walked out of the confessional. I lowered my head, furtively looking to see if a crowd waited to see me, the person who upset the priest. I was flabbergasted that people were still in line waiting to see *this* priest. My penance this time made up for the years of carrying guilt. That priest left an outstanding impact on me forever. I now look at confession and forgiveness as a gift from a loving God. Carrying guilt afterward only weakens our faith. It was the greatest lesson.

I went back to the bench and took out my rosary beads to say my penance. They were clear beads with silver chain links and a matching cross but turned multi-colors when the sun hit them. Al had given me these rosaries as an anniversary gift. A few people at work couldn't understand my thrill in receiving them.

One person said, "Rosaries for your anniversary? I don't see how that kind of a gift would make you happy."

They missed seeing the meaning of this present. My husband didn't go to church, but took the time to look for the right rosary beads for me. He chose them himself. Al had witnessed how much prayer meant to me. His gift gave me hope and faith that he himself was being led to Jesus through conversion.

Cross Mountain faced me as I said my rosaries. The cross on top of the summit was in the distance, the morning sun hitting the Crucifix directly. I had read that the cross weighs 15 tons, is 22 feet tall and was built in honor of 1,933 years since the birth of Christ. It had become a symbol of faith, hope, and charity and a means of penance and conversion, first for the villagers of Medjugorje, and now for the multitude of pilgrims alleged to have had apparitions of the Virgin Mary here.

The sun sent a warm sensation through me as I prayed. Nothing at this moment was as important as the peaceful, private corner where I felt the presence of Our Lady.

Visionaries Jakov, Vicka and Father Slavko

Arlene and I met with our tour group that was walking to the home of the visionary, Jakov, to hear him speak. Jakov Colo was born on March 6, 1971, in Sarajevo. He has had daily apparitions since June 25, 1981. Jakov was married with three children and he lived with his family in Medjugorje. The prayer intention that Our Lady had confided to him was for the sick.

At his home, Jakov and his interpreter were on his front porch waiting at the railing for another group approaching. He was the youngest of the six visionaries and was only ten years old when Our Lady had originally appeared. Jakvo talked about an episode that happened during this youthful period. He and Vicka were taken physically to Heaven, Hell and Purgatory with Our Lady. He was so terrified to know that this was going to occur that he had begged Our Lady to just take Vicka, who was sixteen at the time. Both of them witnessed people in Heaven clothed all in white gowns and weaving baskets.

Jakov didn't wish to give a description about Hell at all. "There are no words to illustrate the horror of it," he alleged. Jakov told us that Purgatory was a dark, murky environment where souls suffer while being purified before entering into Heaven. There are three levels. Souls that have severe sins at the time of death start at the lowest, which is closest to Hell for their suffering. People on Earth are the only ones who can pray to get them out of Purgatory and reach Heaven.

He said, "We're to be prepared for our death at all times."

Jakvo continued by saying he and Vicka vanished for over twenty minutes as family members searched the nearby area for them. I tried to imagine their experience of knowledge that had been obtained from traveling beyond our life with Our Lady. They had all the answers to the questions we were all asking. He ended his story and offered to respond to any questions.

I later discovered that on September 12, 1998, four months after my return home, Jakvo received his tenth secret from Our Lady. She told him he would have one yearly apparition on Christmas Day. The Medjugorje websites had write-ups that he cried for hours from the heartbreak after his last daily apparition with Our Blessed Mother. After seventeen years, he would no longer see Her on a daily basis.

After Jakvo thanked us for coming and prayed over us, groups of pilgrims walked toward Vicka's home. Vicka Ivankovic-Mijatovic was born on September 3, 1964, in Bijakovici. She still had daily apparitions. Our Lady had entrusted nine secrets to her so far. Vicka wrote about her experiences in the book, *Thousand Encounters with the Blessed Virgin Mary in Medjugorje* (1985). Vicka lived in Krehin Gradac near Medjugorje. The prayer intention that Our Lady confided to her was for the sick, the same request as Jakov's.

Fr. Ed Sousa and Vicka

The crowd gathered, standing shoulder to shoulder in the backyard, waiting for Vicka to emerge from the house. The flow of people filled every inch of her property. The individuals who couldn't get through the gate had to listen from the street that was about twenty feet from the driveway.

Vicka came out of a side door on the second floor onto a small balcony. The steep stairs led down to the courtyard and she came halfway down the steps to address everyone. At ground level, people wouldn't have been able to see her through the crowd. Even so the multitude of individuals made it impossible for some to see her. I could spot her when someone standing in front of me changed position.

Vicka was recognized as the "smiling visionary." She seemed to delight in talking to every pilgrim who traveled to Medjugorje. Hundreds of pilgrims came to see her, hoping to be healed.

As Vicka described her daily apparitions with Our Lady, Arlene leaned over and whispered, "Imagine...her eyes have looked right into the eyes of Our Lady!"

I tried to picture something so sacred.

Vicka stated, "Those who follow the Ten Commandments have nothing to worry about, those who love and care for others have the Holy Spirit, and those who are loyal will be shown ways around the danger that looms."

She continued, "God's giving so much time for these apparitions so that all may come to conversion. Our Lady wants to make certain that all people, from all creeds and beliefs, have this opportunity. She can't help anybody who doesn't want to change, who doesn't come back to God, who doesn't put God first. If you don't do this *now*...it will be too late."

Vicka tried to answer as many questions as she could and then proceeded to pray over all of us. It was ten minutes of silence and Arlene thought the prayer time was unusually long in the presence of pilgrims.

The sun blazed down on us. Being stationed in one position for such a length of time, with no shade, caused a young woman in front of us to almost pass out. Someone caught her as she started to fall. A friend supported her while another person poured water over her head. Vicka continued with closed eyes for another ten minutes. When people realized she was done and noticed her leaving to go up the stairs, they started pushing from all directions to climb the steps to try to make contact with her.

We had visited four of the six visionaries which Charlie told us was rare. The last two visionaries weren't in

Medjugorje at this time and we wouldn't be able to meet them. The fifth visionary was Marija Pavlovic-Lunetti who was born on April 1, 1965, in Bijakovici. She still had daily apparitions. Through her, Our Lady gave her messages to the parish and the world. From March 1, 1984, to January 8, 1987, the message was given every Thursday, and since January 1987, on the 25th of every month. Our Lady entrusted ten secrets to her. Marija was married and had three children and lived in Italy and in Medjugorje. The prayer intention that Our Lady confided to her was for the souls in Purgatory.

The sixth visionary is Ivanka Ivankovic-Elez, born on June 21, 1966, in Bijakovici. She was the first visionary to have seen Our Lady. She had daily apparitions until May 7, 1985. On that day, confiding to her the tenth secret, Our Lady told her for the rest of her life, she would have one yearly apparition on June 25th, the anniversary of the apparitions. Ivanka was married, had three children, and she lived with her family in Medjugorje. The prayer intention that Our Lady confided to her was for families.

Before the night's activities took place, Arlene and I went back to the house to get some rest. While we climbed two flights of stairs to get to our room, I was glad we weren't assigned to the third floor. With the combination of stair climbing and the high temperature every day, it was a miracle my health was holding up. All my torment back home being scared of fighting fibrillation on this trip was for nothing.

My bed was right next to a window but with no screens, we encountered bugs and mosquitoes in our bedroom. We kept the casement ajar to take advantage of any small breeze. Both of us felt we would have suffocated with the window fully closed. I took my chances with the mosquito attacks. We found that the best way to keep the mosquitoes out at night was by not keeping our lights on.

Arlene and I never seemed to be able to catch a five minute catnap during the day because of the intense heat. I gathered up a new outfit of dry clothes and headed for a stimulating, ice-cold shower. This was when I discovered the water was shut off at noon and not turned on again until morning. Our clothes stuck to us. I realized that fresh clothes would become wet within hours. I had never before had clothes drenched from sweat and I had a hard time adjusting to the perspiration. I held on all day, imagining refreshing, cold water running down my body.

It seemed worse being inside the room with no air conditioning in the house than being outside so Arlene and I decided to go to the dining room a little early for supper. Before the meal was served, Arlene went to the corner table where Father Whalen was sitting. She explained the gold design she had found in her rosary pouch. He was taken aback as she positioned the little pouch in his hands.

"I understand that if you see something that seems like a miracle, you should get others to confirm it," Arlene said.

He brought the bag up closer to his eyes and studied the strange pattern inside. Father Whalen then turned the tiny pack inside-out to get a better look. Before saying anything to her, he kissed the pouch.

"It's Our Lady holding Baby Jesus!" he remarked.

He was astonished by the small miracle. Everyone around him got curious and came over to see what he was staring at with Arlene. It didn't take long for everyone to witness the same mysterious event.

It was close to 8 p.m. when we finished eating. Arlene wanted to attend the Eucharist Adoration with Father Slavko at the outside gazebo behind St. James Church.

She said, "Wait until you see the love he has for Jesus as he holds the Eucharist during Adoration."

Arriving with only ten minutes to spare, the benches were already three-quarters full. We entered from the side and were lucky to spot two open seats up front. We were on the side of the altar, and I could only see Father Slavko when he stood up from kneeling. Each time he knelt during Adoration, he disappeared from my view.

Adoration with the Eucharist showed him in deep prayer and his eyes never left the Sacrament. He didn't appear to be aware of the thousands of people watching and sharing this blessed moment with him. He wore the same expression of

176

ecstasy on his face that the visionaries had described when they had their apparitions with Our Lady. No one and nothing else mattered to them.

Father Slavko came to the edge of the stage and held the Eucharist up in the air. He made the sign of the cross and then gradually turned to face each individual for a special blessing. Arlene was right about the love he showed for Jesus during the worship hour.

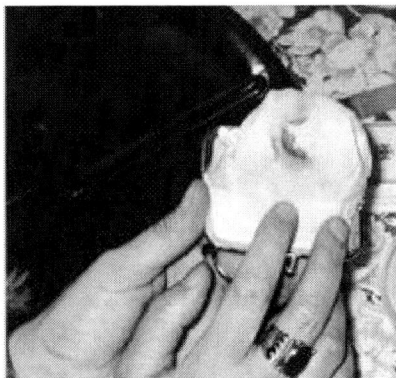

Inside of Arlene's pouch. The dark part is the Baby Jesus leaning against Mary's chest

Father Slavko in Adoration

We walked back to our home around eleven that night. I saved my last climb for the day. By now, I was extremely fatigued. I couldn't remember doing so much in one day. We settled in a while before changing into our pajamas. There was a small amount of water left so we could freshen up. My bed was a welcome sight.

Conversation with Arlene every night calmed me. Our discussions showed me where my life needed changes. Now I had to apply them.

My life had become routine, which is normal for most people. Every weekday, I'd get up at 6 a.m. to go to work and drive forty-five minutes each way. I dealt with tension and stress from phone sales. I arrived home around 6 p.m., ate, showered, and then sat in front of the television until 9 p.m. Al and I would go upstairs to our bedroom only to turn another television set on until the 11 p.m. news ended.

My weekends were filled with housework and errands that couldn't be done during the week. Then there were all the commitments to events, family gatherings or promised favors. Too much to do, too little time, too many missed opportunities to stop and enjoy life itself. Instead of making my time fun, it became work. In a flash, Monday faced me and the pattern started all over again while I watched the clock dictate my schedule.

At the end of the day, I would be so tired that my only desire was to unwind. Mental exhaustion would cause my prayers to be rushed or, too often, skipped completely. Guilt would then overcome me about having pushed God aside. I did manage to find a place for prayer. On a small corner table stood a statue of Our Lady alongside my rosaries and above Her on the wall was a crucifix.

Our Lady had told the visionaries that too much time is spent in front of television and TV games. Conversations between family members have disappeared. Remotes allowed us to jump from one channel to another and people watched two to three programs at once during the commercials. Families used to talk during these breaks. Most of the shows are boring, distasteful, or plain silly, but we watch them anyway just to have what we *think* is entertainment.

In Medjugorje, I never thought about my regular television programs back home. My time was spent talking to strangers, taking walks to enjoy the peace and complete serenity, receiving Jesus daily through the Eucharist, going to confession to free the heaviness in my soul, attending Mass, saying a rosary or simply watching people from all over the world bond.

When I spent time with Jesus and Our Lady in my thoughts, actions and prayers all day, I'd offer my worries up to them. If I fell asleep saying my rosary, Our Lady will understand. My guardian angel will finish the prayer for me.

I saw Medjugorje was about inner peace with Jesus and Mary. A vacation with Al in Hawaii never would have taught me this. I understood why millions of people flocked back to this tiny village again.

Apparitions with Ivan and Mirjana

The next morning, we attended the 7 a.m. Croatian Mass because I wanted to hear the prayers and songs in that language. As we waited outside the church, Arlene and I noticed people staring up at the sky right above the church. A glorious miracle was happening before our eyes. Something was different about the sun. It was so blinding and powerful that I had to put my sunglasses on to look up. A rainbow was forming, which seemed very odd, because no downpour had occurred. Slowly, before our eyes, the spectrum *encircled* the entire sun.

As soon as each end of the rainbow linked together, the sun immediately started to pulsate combining a multitude of colors consisting of pinks, blues, yellow, reds and purple on all sides surrounding the sun. The colors seem to explode from the perimeter.

Arlene looked away from the flaming ball in the sky for a second and remarked, "God's trying to tell us the Church is the center and core of our lives."

The act of God was a gift bestowed on anyone who observed the miracle. How could anyone doubt His existence after seeing this beautiful phenomenon? I had never witnessed or heard of a rainbow that had formed a complete circle. Signs from Heaven were being passed on to pilgrims, and I wondered how many were blind to them. I went to Mass and gave thanks for being there at the right moment to witness the event.

Later that night, the public was invited to join Ivan on Apparition Hill to share an apparition with our Lady at 9:40 p.m. He had already had his 6:40 p.m. apparition but there

179

were times when the Blessed Mother appeared again, inviting the community. Flashlights were required as evening left the pathways in darkness.

We dressed in warmer clothes and brought heavy sweatshirts in case there was a chill in the air by the time the apparition was over. The climb up the hill this time wasn't as difficult for me because the sweltering sun had begun to fade. As I stepped over the rocks in my climb, I looked down and noticed they were covered with sparkling, gold specks. Since I had my backpack, I stopped to pick up a few rocks to take home. The gold dust stuck to my fingers. I was being fussy, picking three and checking them over because of how different they were from any rocks I had ever seen.

On the ascend Arlene brought me to a location where, last year, she had discovered a stone in the shape of Our Lady's face. Returning to the site, she couldn't find the rock.

"I know the stone was right here," she insisted searching the whole area hoping to spot the granite piece.

"I remember you showing me the picture of the stone."

I searched for a rock that might be special in the form of something spiritual but I couldn't find any and we continued on up the hill.

The sunset gave way to another beautiful, clear night. Dusk formed and the sky started to display the glitter of stars in the upper atmosphere. Not once did we have a day with rain to hinder our activities.

People came from all directions to Apparition Mountain to find a place to sit. We had a difficult time trying to settle ourselves because of the jagged rocks. I took a pad of paper from my backpack to write in my journal. This was something I did throughout each day so I wouldn't forget my experiences.

Not far from where we sat, a group of teenage boys played their guitars and sang. Their voices blended together and echoed off the mountain. I noticed a young girl next to me who was using her tape recorder to capture the musical sounds; something I had never thought of bringing. Our Lady had asked Ivan to form a prayer group with the youth in Medjugorje.

By the time we found a place to rest, the crowd had already encircled where Ivan would be perched. It was still light enough to look down the mountain at the quiet little village beneath us. The sun was going down behind the horizon and I thought *when have I ever sat outside to watch a sunset?*

At 9:15 p.m., an hour later, Ivan arrived with his wife, Laureen, and their daughter who looked to be about six years old. I couldn't make their features out because the sun set and the area was covered in darkness. As soon as Ivan and his family joined his group, the boys stopped singing.

Before Our Lady would descend from Heaven to appear to the visionaries, Ivan led us in the rosary and each pilgrim joined in the prayer.

At exactly 9:40 p.m., a boy who was with Ivan announced that Our Lady was appearing. There wasn't a sound or movement on the hill, the world around us fell completely still.

I tried to comprehend the reality that Our Blessed Mother was somewhere in my presence. *She was descended from Heaven to be on Earth with us!* I closed my eyes and prayed from deep within my heart for her to bless my friends and family back home as I openly held all the petitions in my hand.

I selfishly wished for the chance to see or feel my Heavenly Mother. Then without being prepared to experience anything, a tremendous, overpowering fragrance of roses was all around me. It seemed like someone put a field of roses under my nose. The aroma was intense. I knew this was gift from Our Lady, because I could feel Her presence in my soul. There were no roses near us, except at the bottom of the hill.

Not realizing I had had the same sensation, Arlene quickly grabbed my arm. "Smell the roses? This happens when she appears!"

The apparition lasted about six minutes. The interpreter explained to the crowd what message Our Lady had told Ivan. "Our Blessed Mother came down from Heaven and intercedes for our intentions. She prayed for the sick, and for our families back home, and asked us to pray especially for the youth. She blessed us and went up to Heaven with a radiant cross behind Her."

After they heard the message, the crowd broke up and went back down the mountain. I couldn't move after experiencing such a sacred occurrence. I was actually in her presence *the very moment* She appeared! How I'd longed for this experience after reading about these apparitions in my Medjugorje book. My desire was fulfilled beyond anything imaginable.

Arlene sat holding a flashlight for me while I wrote Ivan's words down in my journal. Once I completed my notes, we got up and followed the remaining people down the hill. The pilgrims had their flashlights on and the beams looked like fireflies as we traveled down the steep, rocky trail.

There was only silence along the pathway. I assumed everyone still felt the holiness of being in Our Lady's presence. The scent of the roses stayed with me, and I kept breathing in the sweet aroma.

The next morning, Wednesday, Arlene and I woke up at 7 a.m. to have an early breakfast. We were going to see Mirjana at the Blue Cross where she received her monthly message with Our Lady. The second of each month She appeared to Mirjana on the same roadway as Apparition Hill and only a block away. The lane leading to the area was between two houses. I desperately wanted to get as close to her as we could, but a huge crowd had already formed around where she would be kneeling.

Arlene and I had to settle for sitting on the hill above Mirjana, in between thick, wild rosebushes covered with thorns. The fragrance from the flowers growing on the bluff continuously attracted bugs and bees.

We were there only seconds before Mirjana arrived with her interpreter. He gently motioned for the mob to make room for her to go up to the blue cross. The visionaries were blessed with so much patience, enduring the multitude of people who tried to touch them.

I had to hold the brush back with my hands to watch Mirjana. She arrived with a white, lace veil over her head. She went directly up to the Blue Cross without even looking at a single person.

Her eyes were fixed only on the cross, and I didn't miss the expression of love and endearment on her face as she knelt, filled with anticipation searching for her Heavenly Mother.

Like all of the visionaries, she held her rosaries and started to say them and the surrounding pilgrims joined her, including Arlene and me. No announcement was made that she was having her apparition, but when she lifted her head toward the top of the cross, I sensed the miracle happening. She suddenly was moving her lips but her words couldn't be heard.

Nothing distracted her. Her gaze never stopped looking up while receiving her apparition. I took the petitions out of my backpack again and placed them on my lap, closed my eyes, and prayed for everyone's healing.

I stared back at Mirjana. Tears ran down her face when the apparition ended. The love she felt for Our Lady had to be beyond anything we felt for another person after seeing and talking with Her. Returning back to the earthly things must have been difficult and painful for any of the visionaries.

Mirjana told her interpreter what the message was for the world and left. She said Our Lady blessed all our petitions and families back home. This was my second time in Our Lady's presence. What a blessing.

Arlene praying at the Blue Cross behind Our Lady's Statue

Climbing Cross Mountain

After Mirjana's apparition, Arlene and I headed back to attend the morning Mass. I felt quite tired after so many days filled with activities and late hours. Today our group was going to climb Cross Mountain. This was the biggest goal I wanted to complete on my trip. It was so important for me to be able to ascend to the top and look down at the little village of Medjugorje. This mountain was bigger than Apparition Hill where Our Lady had appeared to the visionaries. This location was the most meaningful site in my video, and I longed to sit on the highest point of the summit. My trip to Medjugorje wouldn't be fulfilled without this accomplishment.

We ate a light meal, and I became aware of my worst fear… fibrillation. *Oh, God! Not now. Don't let this happen to me. I have to climb the mountain.* All week I'd been in perfect health. *Why now? Why would Jesus let this happen?*

I took a firm hold of Arlene's arm and looked at her with complete fright on my face.

I pulled her aside. "Oh my God, Arlene, I'm having fibrillation."

She calmly replied, "Don't panic. We'll go to Mass and pray for your heart to get back to normal."

Charlie called the group together and announced, "Usually we climb the mountain early in the morning, but the day is going to be extremely hot, reaching close to one hundred degrees. Let's reschedule and meet at 4 p.m. at the house. The day is yours until then."

This'll give me all day for the fibrillation to stop, I prayed.

I took one of the tranquilizers my doctor had advised me to take. Sometimes the episodes lasted ten straight hours. Arlene and I headed straight for the services. My mind only focused on my racing heart.

Arlene looked at me and said, "I have no doubt this is the work of the devil. He works on people's health to keep them away from the greatest desire that they want to achieve in Medjugorje."

"Well, he's doing a great job right now."

I prayed at Mass and my irregular heartbeat didn't go away. We went back to the house and met our group on the front patio. They were in the middle of deciding who would read at each station going up the mountain and which person would carry the cross. I volunteered to read at the second and seventh station.

Stations of the Cross was a devotion consisting of prayers said before a series of fourteen pictures or carvings representing successive incidents during Jesus' passage from Pilate's house to his crucifixion at Calvary. The object of the Stations was to help the faithful to make a spiritual pilgrimage of prayer, through meditating upon the chief scenes of Christ's sufferings and death. This worship has become one of the most popular devotions for Roman Catholics.

I wondered if I'd be able to even make the trip. The more I worried about my condition, the worse my fibrillation got. I struggled to breathe normally.

I said to Arlene, "I'm not going to be able to go. If I can't climb stairs at home during my attacks, how am I going to achieve climbing an actual *mountain*?"

"We'll worry about your situation when the time comes."

The heat was going to make my heart complications worse, and the climb would take two hours in the sweltering sun to reach the top.

Arlene tried to get me to relax. By now everyone in the party knew of my dilemma. I went upstairs to my bedroom to get some rest, hoping my difficulties with my breathing would stop. Arlene went shopping so I could be alone to get some sleep.

I slept for an hour and after opening my eyes, I could still feel the fibrillation. My clothes were soaked from sleeping in the heat. The windows were closed, only adding to the high temperature in our room. No more water was available to take a shower and I felt frustrated. If I could have cooled off, some of the stress would come off my heart. This was the worst day of heat with a high temperature slightly over a hundred degrees.

Supper was going to be at 3 p.m. that day because of the scheduled journey. I wouldn't be able to eat a full meal because the food wouldn't digest before the climb and could cause more trouble in my breathing from exerting myself. *Oh Lord, what a test.*

Burying my embarrassment, I went up to Father Whalen and told him of my condition. I expressed my fear of not being able to go with the group. He felt the same as Arlene, agreeing my health problem was the devil working to keep me from fulfilling the climb.

Father asked if everyone could pray over me, and I welcomed the idea. The pack held hands and circled around me. As Father started the grace, I realized the prayer was Anointing of the Sick, said at the last rites for the dying. I heard the words, "To heal and forgive sins since your last confession." Father Whalen continued to bless each individual in the group for their trip to Cross Mountain.

A short gentleman in his fifties with gray hair and wearing jeans came over to me and said, "I can relate to what you're going through. During my first trip to Medjugorje, I had an angina attack trying to climb the mountain and swore I was going to die. Halfway to the top, my symptoms somehow passed."

Arlene suggested that the two of us take a taxi to the mountain to avoid as much walking as possible. Cross Mountain wasn't that far from the house, but walking any distance with my heart skipping and racing wasn't only exhausting, but made it hard to breathe.

I got into the cab thinking about what a huge mistake this might be with doing so much physical activity in my condition.

I felt that pushing my desire for this climb would only cause a serious need for me to go to the hospital.

The taxi drove past the rest of the gang walking and within two minutes we arrived at the foot of the hill. My fears rose higher. I looked up at the mountain and realized the path wasn't a gradual ascend; in fact, the scale was steeper than Apparition Hill. Thick sticks resembling staffs were available to help people go up the trail. I took one in case I needed the support.

I had concentrated so much on my heart troubles that I had forgotten to bring water with me. I looked around and noticed everyone else had bottles connected to their belts. I tried desperately to make off that I was in control of my fibrillation. Although my heart bounced inside my chest, out of normal rhythm, making it difficult even to talk. I fought back tears from fright and stress. If I broke down and cried, I would completely lose control of the situation.

A heavy set man who wore mountain boots approached me. "Try going to just one or two stations and then come back down."

I knew he meant well but how could I go that far and then turn around? I *had* to reach the top.

Arlene took me aside, "Watch me. I'm going to show you how to go up the mountain. Take each step slowly, like you're actually in slow motion. Don't rush your stride. I learned this technique with my last trip here. People make the mistake of trying to go up too fast and not resting."

Arlene stayed in front of me so I couldn't pass her. Slowly, I put one foot in front of the other. We would take a step and then hesitate before taking the next one. I could now feel my heart beating irregularly in my throat. I was wondering why on Earth I was doing this with a heart problem. *Was I insane?*

I imagined myself sitting on top, absorbing the whole wonder of this miracle in Medjugorje.

We arrived at the second station and my turn came to read. I said each word slowly and steadily so no one would hear how out of breath I was. The group began to depart for the next station when Rocco a gray haired Italian, came up to me and

187

poured his bottled water all over my head. He gave up his whole supply to give me relief from the heat.

This man didn't think twice about what he had lost for himself. His only concern was to make me comfortable. Moved by his kindness, I took his hands and gave a smile with my eyes full of tears. No words had to be exchanged between us.

I kept pulling air into my chest, trying to regulate the fibrillation. I needed to rest but didn't want to fall behind. Finally, a point came where I decided to pull away mentally from just thinking about myself. I started to offer my suffering up for the Souls in Purgatory, as Dad had taught me.

I knew Father Whalen had just given me the last rites to start my journey and my confession had been heard a few days before, so my soul had been cleansed from sin. If God decided to take me during my climb, I felt spiritually ready.

As ridiculous as it may sound, I wondered how my family would get my body back home. It was crazy how many things went through my mind in minutes while I tried to reach the top of the mountain. I understood that Jesus was only interested in our souls, not our bodies. That was where all our love and faith was contained.

My father entered my thoughts. He had wanted to travel to Medjugorje as much as I did. Eight years had passed since his death. My sister, Leona, had prayed the rosary and attended Mass for him every single morning for over a year. She received peace in knowing he was home with God. I wanted the same peace within my soul. I needed to heal my heart. Why else would I be here? What was the reason for my calling?

God, if he's not with you now, please take him home when I get to the top. Let this be my journey for him spiritually to save his soul.

This was going to be my gift to my father. I ignored my discomfort and kept looking up at the enormous, cement cross facing me on the peak. I felt the presence of Jesus in my heart.

I read again at the seventh station and started up the hill. Once we reached the eleventh station, I felt my heart jump back into a normal rhythm. My pain was replaced by a peaceful feeling. I had put my life and trust into God's hands and my health was restored.

Why did I doubt Him?

Tears overcame me when I realized what Jesus was trying to teach me. I truly believe that at one time or another, we'll all suffer, whether it's mentally or physically. It's our punishment from the sins of Adam and Eve. Jesus waits for us to offer up our suffering, in place of His for us, and have faith in Him. With my heart problem gone, I felt the blessing that was bestowed on me.

I looked at Arlene. "I'm fine now. My problem left as soon as I offered my suffering up."

She hugged me, looking relieved.

Nearing my final steps, the huge cross appeared in front of me, and the others were hugging and laughing with excitement.

I passed by them and left Arlene to be by myself. I walked past the famous, stupendous cross and went straight to a small, stained wooden cross on the other side. The Crucifix was weather-beaten and stood about two feet tall. I felt a strong force leading me there to kneel and pray.

I wondered why there, instead of falling at the large concrete cross, the one I had longed to reach. I felt humble and small looking at this cross that was completely isolated. Jesus had led a simple life, and I felt a private connection to Him at this location.

During my prayers, I knew in my heart that my father was in Heaven. I received the peace that Leona already had. Maybe that was why she wasn't called, and I was.

Did I need this journey to Medjugorje to find this contentment?

When I ended giving thanks to Jesus for helping me finish my journey, I looked for Arlene. Such a remarkable woman; she knew when to let me be by myself. A week's friendship and we both understood the importance of being isolated to become connected to the Holy Spirit. That's the secret: being alone in prayer. If you're patient, you *will* feel Him.

Arlene and I sat together silently on the Cross Mountain steps looking down at the village. My eyes and heart were awestruck witnessing the sight I had longed to see. Nothing else on Earth could have been more of a blessing or gift from Jesus and Mary.

Our group gathered in front of the giant cross to take pictures. There was so much tranquility in my body and mind that I had no desire to leave my spot to join them. The pictures were in my soul. What I witnessed would never be replaced or topped by any other trip, not even Hawaii.

An hour passed before Arlene and I joined friends to start down Cross Mountain. I picked up my staff and waved my left hand in the onward motion like Moses for them to follow me. It was hard to believe that I was now skipping down the path.

Everyone laughed after sharing in my struggle coming up the mountain. They saw me joyful after a long tour of pain and suffering. Maybe it's similar to the agony we have to go through before entering into Heaven. My misery showed me God's love. The most important desire of my trip was accomplished. Satan was once again defeated!

When we reached the bottom of the mountain, we all walked to a restaurant directly across the street. Everyone refreshed themselves with cold drinks. Exhaustion took over after fighting to control my physical and mental state of health throughout the whole day. Other pilgrims started to walk back to the houses or called for a taxi. I joined in, sharing a ride because my knees felt like rubber. There was no more energy left in me to walk the short distance back.

Final Days in Medjugorje

I woke up Friday morning, facing my last full day at Medjugorje. My flight was leaving Saturday and already I felt the sadness and depression. I went to the 10 a.m. Mass absolutely heartbroken knowing there wouldn't be another morning to sit in this sacred church. How could I go back to my church, with only one priest on the altar and many empty pews?

Arlene and I finally decided to visit the gift stores to look for holy items. The store behind the church displayed the beautiful statues. I made sure my family members would receive a rosary blessed by Father Whalen. Some of my family members have left the Church but I would leave their conversion in the Hands of God in His time and way.

After our visit to the gift store, we walked around the village. Eddie came upon us with a warm and proud smile on his face.

"I brought something really special for the two of you," he said.

He had come across a medal that was extremely close to the image of Mary holding baby Jesus that was embedded into Arlene's rosary pouch. The medal would always remind us of the gift given to Arlene from Our Lady.

After shopping, I decided to go back to the house early and start packing. This way I would have no anxiety from having to think about the chore all day. I climbed the stairs with no enthusiasm. The combination of not wanting to leave Medjugorje and knowing Arlene and Eddie were staying longer made my departure hard to accept.

After getting my things in order, I spent the day praying and watching the pilgrims going in and out of St. James Church. Supper was special since this was the last night for most of us. The dining area was extremely noisy with everyone talking all at once discussing their week's events. Individuals were passing out their names, addresses and phone numbers on paper. I could now understand how friendships developed on a pilgrimage.

After a very relaxing meal, Penny joined us for a walk around the area. She was a quiet spoken woman with a blondish, Dutch-style hairdo who became deeply involved with her church after losing her faith. Arlene and Penny talked about the miracles that they had witnessed the year before on their trip to Medjugorje. The hot sun was setting and there was a motionless feeling in the air. My eyes acted like a camera, trying to take pictures of every inch of Medjugorje so the sights would last forever in my mind.

Arlene wanted to show me the cemetery at the far end of St. James Church. The graves were all above the ground, encased in cement monuments like the ones we had passed as we had come into the village. The area was peaceful and serene, with only the sound of the birds. The three of us started making our way back when suddenly the aroma of roses filled the air.

I stopped dead in my tracks, "Oh! Smell the roses?"

There were no roses in the area. Penny and Arlene didn't smell any. The fragrance was the same strong scent as on Apparition Hill when Our Lady appeared to Ivan.

Penny just smiled, "It must be a gift just for you from the Blessed Mother before you leave."

I had difficulty keeping my emotions together with the sorrow that filled my whole body. I wanted to wrap up the whole village and take it home. I knew the same old habits and problems not found in Medjugorje would be facing me on my return.

I ached to go home and have our world turn back the way we lived in earlier times. Marriages were entered into without the sex first, brides went down the church aisle in white for a reason, parents said no to a child if it was in their best interest or safety, and they weren't trying to be friends to their children, they weren't allowed in the room during adult conversations, and we learned to respect someone who may not be the same race or faith. Family spent time together.

"However, take care and be earnestly on your guard not to forget the things which your own eyes have seen, nor let them slip from your memory as long as you live, but teach them to your children and to your children's children" (Deuteronomy 4:9).

I believe that Our Lady wants all the pilgrims, who had come to Medjugorje, to go home and spread peace and help to convert others so they'll return to their faith. Medjugorje shows us in our hearts what's really important in our lives and not to focus on the material things. When people back home see us doing good for others, they may want to follow. We have to keep God's name in our speech, actions and writings.

Visionaries all over the world are trying to save us by informing the world what they're actually seeing and hearing from Our Lady or Jesus. They have seen everything that's here and beyond. If we listen and do what's asked of us, which isn't much, we'll end up at the same doors where the visionaries will be at the end of time. What more could we ask for than to spend our lives with God in peace and happiness after our death?

We all entered this world alone and we'll leave it alone. It's up to each individual to decide what to do with their own life because no one else can decide this for us. No one can save you from Hell except yourself. If you believe in God, your soul will be saved. The existence of God and Heaven will not disappear just because you may not believe in them. God's own words are, *"I Am...That I Am" (Exodus, 3.14).*

Medjugorje has given me a renewal of life. Time will tell me why I was called here. I'll have to sit and listen quietly for God to talk to me when I'm alone. I felt my spiritual changes deep within my soul. My pilgrimage showed me how I can live without the material things. This, I think is the answer.

193

We belong to God and need to believe and have confidence in Him.

We have to open our hearts every single day, with no fear, for Him to enter our souls and lead us to Heaven. You don't believe? That's all right. God already knows your weaknesses and everything else about you. He's aware of our wants, needs and desires. Prayer is just talking to God as one would to a friend. Ask the Holy Spirit to come and help you understand your faith. Pray and you'll feel Him.

"God is our refuge and our strength an ever-present help in distress" (Psalm 46:2).

Prayer slows down your fast-paced life. Difficulties in decision-making will fall in place with the answers. Peace will come to you and turmoil and despair will leave. We have to come to the realization soon that our time on Earth is short, but our life after death is forever. Where do you want your soul to go? Until our world ends, God is merciful by giving us Purgatory.

The three of us walked quietly back to the village and headed to Papillon Cafe Restaurant owned by Viktor. This was our favorite restaurant to get our nightly ice cream sundae treat. The café was full because so many were leaving the next morning. No one wanted the night to end. The three of us couldn't find a seat until Eddie waved us over to a spot he had saved.

I enjoyed sitting outside late at night under the stars. The deafening laughter and voices were strident from all the pent-up excitement and the feelings of restlessness that was here in all of us.

I didn't want the night to end, but fatigue was catching up with me. Every day was long. We woke around 7 a.m. and rarely went to bed earlier than midnight. Tonight, once I hit the bed, my trip was over.

Finally around eleven, we headed upstairs to our room. I was relieved to know my clothes were already packed. The bus was going to arrive in the morning around seven, so breakfast would be early. My nightly conversation with Arlene wasn't long because of my need for sleep. We tried to squeeze as much talk as we could before drifting off.

I woke up at 5 a.m. to the sound of suitcases bouncing down the stairs. The noise acted as an alarm clock for those of us about to leave Medjugorje. The men in the group were busy collecting the travel bags that had been left outside each door.

I tried to look happy, but the sorrow absolutely engulfed me. *How am I going to leave?* I asked God to forgive me for being so selfish wanting to stay away from my family longer.

Arlene joined me for an early breakfast that was prepared for the ones leaving. I had no real appetite, but ate a boiled egg with a piece of Italian bread. I put an apple in my backpack since my travel home was going to be long. Everyone ran around the dining area saying goodbye to those staying behind and to the family who had served us the whole week.

Every step toward the bus was forced and my smile felt pasted on me. After all the pieces of luggage were counted, the group started up the bus steps to depart. Arlene and I kissed each other goodbye, acting like the torment wasn't bothering either of us. The tears were ready to come, so I hugged her fast and went on the bus.

I sat by a window and looked out at the village for one last time. I was leaving a place with so much love and tranquility. I waved to Arlene until the bus disappeared around the corner.

We passed St. James Church and I thought, *If only I was alone so I could cry and let this pain escape*—it was choking me. I had now learned what the true feelings were after a pilgrimage and had come to know why everyone wanted to return to Medjugorje. I wondered if I would ever come back.

As we started to pull out of the village, I could see Cross Mountain in the distance to my left. I gazed out the window and lovingly spoke to Our Lady, *You called me and gave me this wonderful gift of making my faith stronger, and now leaving is too hard. Please help me bring this knowledge home to my friends and family.*

I stared at the holy mountain, knowing my biggest dream had come true climbing to its peak. I was now comfortable with leaving because I felt my father deep within me. Dad's presence would always be in Medjugorje. *You're home now, Dad. I did this for both of us. Serenity will always follow me knowing that you're in Heaven with our Father and Walter.*

I had come to Medjugorje thinking I needed answers after my father's death, but now realized I needed a healing heart in order to be able to say goodbye to him.

"Have no anxiety at all, but in everything, by prayer and petition, with thanksgiving, make your request known to God. Then the peace of God that surpasses all understanding will guard your hearts and minds in Christ Jesus." (Philippians 4:6-7)

We were an hour and a half into the ride to the airport when the bus came to a complete stop. It wasn't completely daybreak, and I couldn't see where we were. The bus driver opened the door for a soldier to come aboard. Since I had sat at the back of the bus, I couldn't hear what the driver and soldier said to each other.

As the soldier started down the middle of the aisle, I notice he had a rifle over his shoulder. When he came closer to my seat, I realized by his uniform that he wasn't an American. His attire had the colors of dark green and yellow blend mixing together. This had to be official business because we were all asked to hand our passports over to him. He had a firm military expression with no smile.

I looked out the window and noticed three more soldiers with rifles outside the bus. I felt uneasy; after all, it was wartime. After he had collected all the passports, he went out to the other soldiers. I quickly leaned over to a man across the aisle and asked if this was a normal procedure.

The gentleman remarked, "I've been here a few times and never had this happen."

I later learned we were at the International border crossing between Bosnia-Herzegovina and Croatia. This was where passports were required to be shown as requested. Sometimes the soldiers stopped buses at random.

Within minutes, the bus started to move again, and the passports were passed back to us. I felt foolish being scared over normal procedures. After all, during a war you hear about people being taken off buses and shot; again, negative thoughts. I had to remember Our Lady promised to take care of the pilgrims.

The sun was coming up and the scenery was beautiful along the Adriatic seacoast. The bus went at a slow pace, bouncing over the same unpaved roads we had traveled coming into Medjugorje.

I became conscious of the fact that I loved my family but the love I felt for Medjugorje, wasn't something from this earth—emotions were from Heaven. It's a love that became so deep inside my heart and soul, I wanted to reach out and embrace the spiritual fire above anything else in my life, even my loved ones. I felt the closeness of Jesus and Mary more than I ever could have imagined.

Medjugorje is a *sampler* of Heaven. We learn and feel what awaits us if we turn to God and give Him the worship He is entitled to. We should treat all strangers as though they were Jesus standing in front of us. If I had a choice as to where I would like to be at the time of my death, it would have been here in this little village—it's the closest I will ever be to Paradise.

Once we left Split, there would only be one layover at Newark Airport. I spent the eight hours on the flight reading books about Medjugorje. I felt totally lost, traveling back without Arlene. She had become my dearest friend. A few hours of sleep would have been a blessing, but my insides were on high speed, reminiscing about my week's pilgrimage.

I was thankful that our flight to New Jersey felt fast. As we approached the runway, the plane came in with the left wing slanted towards the ground.

My mind was yelling, *Straighten out...Straighten out.*

Smiles from relief were exchanged along with nervous laughs and loud claps as we touched down safely. Suddenly, passengers crowded the aisle to grab their belongings from the overhead bins. They were already standing before the plane had come to a complete stop at the terminal. I wondered why they had stood so soon, with nowhere to go. We were now jammed together without being able to move.

197

People from our group were going in different directions leaving Newark to go home. Many said goodbye fast so the others could catch their connecting flight.

As I boarded my last flight to Boston, I took comfort in knowing there was only an hour and a half left before Al would meet me at Logan Airport. I couldn't wait for the reunion. He would probably not be able to see the changes in me: they were all in my private memories. How would he understand? He's not spiritual and would never be able to comprehend the blessings that were given to me. I wasn't the same person returning home. So much of me was left in Medjugorje.

When I came off the plane, I could see Al waiting at the gate. We had been separated for a week and my heart melted when I saw his smile. My embrace came from the heart as we hugged and kissed. I had become an independent flyer.

Instantly, things around me started to revert to what I considered to be normal but fast-paced. People started pushing, shoving and bumping into us as they rushed to meet their scheduled flights or as they tried to get into line to collect their baggage. No one cared that they were cutting in front of others. Impatient travelers swore as they tried to retrieve their suitcases or search for their lost belongings.

I had just left Medjugorje where there was nothing but constant peace and respect for strangers sharing their space. Someone in need was helped without even thinking twice about their action. There was no rushing in Medjugorje. The village was engulfed in the sounds of prayer, music from St. James Church, and the echo of birds. My eyes filled, thinking about what I had just left behind.

Al put my large suitcase into the trunk of the car and we drove out of the airport. The traffic was bumper to bumper through the Callahan Tunnel. Al joined the maniac drivers on Route 93 to go home to Rochester. Cars passed on the right and left of us. One minute he had to drive at a high rate of speed to keep up with the traffic and then we were in a line of cars showing nothing but brake lights as far as the eye could see.

How can so many people be on the road at once? Where are they all going? What's their rush? *I don't want to be back here.* Al would never identify with what I felt. All the muscles in my neck tightened as the traffic came at us from all directions. I felt sick to my stomach watching how drivers became insane behind the wheel of a car. People would cut us off, show hatred in their eyes, and swear at us.

I could feel the wonderful peace and tranquility that I had brought back come to an end. At the same time this was all happening, Al was smiling and talking to me but I wasn't listening to what was being said. I tried to study the life I was returning to. How did the world get this way without me ever noticing it?

The further we got from Boston, the further I felt from Medjugorje. I wanted to go back where this commotion didn't exist. This wasn't the time to explain this to Al, so I sat back and tried to go along with the fast flow.

Changes in My Life

Sunday morning, I woke up to see a new addition in our backyard next to the fireplace. Just as Arlene predicted, Al had bought a beautiful statue of Our Lady ensconced in a grotto. He was very proud of himself and my happiness only added to his delight. He described all the running around that occurred at different locations until he found one with the perfect, beautiful details on her face. I was touched that he had searched so hard for the right statue to present to me.

Returning to work filled me with a sense of loss. I struggled to get back to the working environment but I felt caged for eight hours when I had been free in Medjugorje to pray wherever and whenever without any outside distractions. I understood why people gave up all their worldly goods to live in Medjugorje. My peace and calmness were disappearing.

I passed out gifts from my trip to my close friends at work. I gave out medals, prayer cards, rosaries and pictures. The girls took me out to lunch because they wanted to hear about my journey. I couldn't believe everyone's excitement. We all had different religious beliefs, but I explained how Medjugorje was for people of all faiths. God wants all his children around the whole world to be saved.

After lunch, I rushed over to see Maryanne and asked how Shawn was doing. She said he joined a baseball league and was making plans to marry. What a miracle.

My first thought was, *another miracle like the ones Dad had talked about.*

Debbi Bettencourt came into my office a few months after my return. She informed me she was pregnant. This had been her request to Our Lady in her petition. She had never told anyone that she had a few miscarriages in the past. She delivered twin girls named Maddy and Ally—a double blessing. I called them the *Medjugorje Miracle Babies.*

Val Poitras, our daughter Lynne's father-in-law, had his prostate cancer cured after giving me his petition. His wife, Georgette, had placed the silver medal that I'd given her in the lobster-claw clasp of her sterling silver bracelet. Within days the clasp turned gold. A jeweler tried buffing the gold off. He had no explanation as to why he couldn't return the clasp to the original silver.

Less than a year after my trip, the chain links of my father's traveling rosaries turned gold. I called Leona to tell her about my discovery as soon as it happened.

Before I could share the excitement, she cut me off. Her voice was shaking as she explained an event to me, "You're the only one I can tell this story to because no one else would believe me. I had the most incredible experience just now."

She had been under a lot of stress with their lumber business in Buzzard Bay and feared she was on the verge of a breakdown. Five years earlier, her husband, Bob, had gone back to their home in Punxsutawney, Pennsylvania to run their mattress store. This separation put a lot of strain on Leona who was left to handle the lumberyard with just our brother, Bill, as the lumberyard manager.

She continued, "I was sitting in the backroom doing the bookkeeping, and my nerves were ready to jump out of my body. Without any warning, I was physically lifted into another place. It looked like Jerusalem, and I was standing in a crowd on a cobble street.

"This wasn't a dream, I was living it. A man passed by and brushed his gown against me. It was Jesus! I didn't see His face because His back was to me. I felt Him. His gown was the same cream color as Dad's rosaries, and His brown hair was long. As soon as the gown touched me, a tremendous peace came over me. All my pressure seemed to lift from me. I actually felt Jesus! Please don't think I'm crazy," she said with uncontrollable sobs.

Once she calmed down and stopped crying, I said, "Leona, I believe you. Let me tell you about Dad's rosaries." When I completed the story, I said, "Isn't it odd for our two supernatural events to have happened on the same day?"

When I saw her a few days later, I gave her our father's rosaries. She kept them a short time, claiming I was meant to keep them because of the spiritual changes occurring in my life since Dad's death.

September 11, 1999, our daughter Carol, agreed with the family that it was time to get her son, Jordan, nine years old, and her daughter, Julia, seven years old, baptized. Carol and her husband, Bill, had been separated, and she was living with us. Al's other daughter, Lynne, and her husband Ron, were going to be the Godparents.

Baptism is a religious sacrament marked by the symbolic application of water to the head or immersion of the body into water and resulting in admission of the recipient into the community of Christians; a ceremony by which one is initiated, purified, or given a name.

Monsignor Perry from the St. John Neumann Church in East Freetown was going to celebrate the religious sacrament. It was the first time we had entered this church. I attended St. Rose of Lima Church in Rochester only one minute down the street from our home.

When we entered the narthex, I noticed a picture of Our Lady on the wall. It was the same as the ones sold in Medjugorje.

I looked at Al and said, "This is going to be our church."

I felt deep down that this was a sign of where we belonged.

As the baptism proceeded with Monsignor Perry, I prayed deeply, "Please, Holy Spirit, come down upon all of us. Bless our whole family and bring them back to church. Help Al receive the desire to start attending Mass with me. Let Carol get through her painful divorce."

I prayed for so many people to return to God; including my daughters, siblings, brothers and their children.

Al liked Monsignor Perry right away. He also loved the fact that the church had air conditioning. Lynne and Ron mentioned that they attended the 8 a.m. Mass every Sunday and invited us to join them. Right away my prayers were answered when Al and Carol both showed an interest in going.

What a joyous morning, when Sunday arrived and everyone was getting ready for church. George Martin was a parishioner who passed out the weekly bulletin at the door. He became a very important person in our lives, pulling us closer to this church.

It was such a blessed gift to see the whole family sitting together in the pew. When Holy Communion time arrived, everyone started down the aisle to receive. No one was conscious that they hadn't been to confession. I knew Al hadn't gone in years. This wasn't the time to explain this to them so I put their decision to receive in God's hands. The last thing I wanted to do was to turn them away from church when they were turning back to their faith.

Coffee and donuts were served in the church hall weekly, after Mass. Monthly breakfasts were also offered. Al was really impressed, thinking this would be something good for the family to share. He especially liked the idea of coffee since he drank so much of it. I laughed. *If it takes coffee and air conditioning to get him to church...let it be, God.* All the parishioners were friendly and sincere about caring for others. I prayed my husband would continue to go to church and not have this be a one-time event attended out of curiosity.

The summer came and George invited us to help out with the yearly church chicken barbecue. To my surprise, Al accepted without thinking twice. George enlisted us into the St. John Neumann's Couples Club. What a wonderful group of people. Once a month, a committee would schedule entertainment for the members. We would take numerous trips to the Foxwoods Casino, shows, dinners, and bowling. Our club ended routinely at Chuck and Julie Millington's yard in August for a cookout and pool party, and again after our next meeting the following year in June.

Father's Day, we attended Mass and were honored to be chosen by George to bring the offering of bread and wine up to the altar. I couldn't believe such a blessing was being bestowed on us this special day. As we presented the offering to the priest, I couldn't hide the tears of happiness. Medjugorje was working its graces and miracles on us as a couple. Never would I have pictured Al going to church, never mind going down the aisle on Father's Day, no less.

Unexpectedly, one night, Carol decided to go back to her husband in Maine. It had been a year of constant court battles. She gave us the story that she was taking the kids out to supper and a late movie. They didn't come home that night.

It was not like Carol to stay out all night with her kids and I told Al my vibes were strong that she went back to Bill. This would have been the second time she had left and returned to him. I'd been praying the rosary, day after day, for her to get her life together and for God to bring someone who would love her instead of watching her as she struggled with her marriage. I was afraid that her problems that made her leave him would only return.

Al called me at work with the news that I had feared; Carol was back in Maine with Bill. The news affected me so much that I had to leave work. We had been trying to help her put the pieces back in her life…and the goal wasn't reached again.

When this happened, I questioned my own faith: why did God let this happen? Why did she go back to him? I wasn't praying for this. It took a few months for me to realize that God did answer my prayers. He answered me in His time and way.

I prayed for her to be happy and Carol was. The results just didn't happen the way I wanted them. My way was with someone else, so she wouldn't be hurt again. I had to let go and let God decide what was best for her. After all, wasn't that what I prayed for?

On November 24, 2000, Father Slavko Barbaric died, at the age of fifty-eight, in Medjugorje. He was saying the rosary, leading a multitude of pilgrims on the journey up Cross Mountain. Calmly, he had sat down to rest and then passed away. For nineteen and a half years, he had traveled throughout the whole world teaching prayer and the love of Jesus and Mary. What a loss to all of us.

In December of 2000, Arlene, Al and I went to LaSalette in Attleboro to see the Christmas decorations. We weren't aware that Bishop Sean O'Malley from Fall River, Massachusetts was going to say and give the shrine a blessing before turning on the lights for the holiday. This was Al's first time hearing him speak. He loved the bishop's gentleness and his strong, clear voice. Bishop O'Malley reminded me of Jesus when he came down the church aisle wearing sandals and carrying a staff. It was a Millennium Mass and we were told if confession was made before the New Year, all our sins of the past would be forgiven. Arlene and I went but Al stayed behind. I had to let him handle his own inner healing.

A few weeks later, Al secretly went back to LaSalette Shrine to have his confession heard, his first time in over thirty years. Our Lady was working miracles beyond my imagination with my husband. *How powerful is prayer?*

May of 2001, Maryanne left the customer service department and came to my office with the sad news that Shawn had died from his cancer. He had lived two more years after my return from Medjugorje. I was so saddened after praying so hard for this stranger who had entered my heart. I accepted his passing as God's will.

Shawn's wake was in Taunton which was about a forty-minute drive from our home. I had an uncontrollable desire to attend for reasons unknown to me. I'd never been to a wake where I didn't know the deceased or a member of the family. During the whole time driving there alone, I debated about turning around and going back home.

At 4 p.m., with the late afternoon sun still strong, I entered the Capro-Hathaway Funeral Home parking lot. Teenagers and young adults sat outside talking. They looked shocked and heartbroken over losing their friend.

I entered the door to the funeral home and tried to blend into the line leading up to Shawn's casket. He had only been in his early twenties. I wanted to see what he looked like to connect to him—but the coffin was closed. I was disappointed that I would be unable to see his face. I knelt in front of the casket and I noticed a picture of him on top. His red hair caught my attention.

When Shawn got married, I had bought a picture titled *Forgiven* from LaSalette Shrine as a wedding gift to him. The picture showed a young boy with red hair in jeans wearing a white t-shirt. His eyes were closed as he leaned the back of his limp body and head against the chest of Jesus. His hand was hanging down by his side, holding a hammer. Jesus held the boy up in His arms.

Instantly, I saw the same red hair on Shawn as the boy in that picture had. Shawn looked like the boy who needed God's strength to hold him up. After his death, his wife couldn't look at the picture because she only saw death. His mother and father took the photo and hung it up in their home.

Shawn was no longer a stranger in my soul. After saying a short prayer, I went over to his wife in the family line to introduce myself. She demonstrated no interest in me as I tried explaining who I was. She was confused and in pain and I was a stranger.

When I mentioned taking the envelope with Shawn's hair to Medjugorje, I heard someone in the background say, "I know her!"

Shawn's mother stepped out from the family line and took my hand, introducing herself. I could feel the heartfelt emotions as she thanked me for coming. We had never met, but Maryanne had connected us by telling me about his mother's prayers throughout his prolonged illness. I expressed how very sorry I was with her son's death. I could only imagine how she felt losing a child.

She said sincerely, "God gave us two more years with him after you took his hair in an envelope on your trip to Medjugorje."

His father couldn't come to me, but I went to him and gently held his hands before I left. I hoped my appearance gave his parents some comfort, knowing I cared about their loss.

Getting to my car, I knew there was closure with Shawn. This was my way of letting go and saying goodbye to him. God has His reasons beyond our ever knowing why or when certain souls are called back to Him earlier in life than others.

Church Sex Scandal

Since the mid 1990's, more than 130 people came forward regarding sexual abuse in the Catholic Church. The scandal was kept quiet and low-key by Church officials. We turned on the television, read the newspaper or listened to the radio, and we discussed the topic. In early 2002, the Boston Globe covered a series of criminal prosecutions of five Roman Catholic priests of sexual abuse of minors by Catholic priests. The wrongdoing was blown wide open by the media.

This was when I realized why Mirjana, while I was on my pilgrimage in 1998, had announced to our tour group that Our Lady asked the world to pray for our priests. She knew how strong Satan had become and that the Church would be tested.

The public and parishioners wanted punishment for all priests. Victims demanded to be compensated, along with having the priests publicly admit to their actions and to ask for forgiveness.

Many were angry and repulsed by the Church. Officials not only knew about the sexual abuse, but had done nothing about the priest's actions. Priests could have been sent to monasteries for solitary punishment, with heavy counseling, not only for the offender, but also for the victims. If they had made these changes, their concern would have helped prevent priests from having any further contact with children. Instead, they positioned them in other parishes, only to have them repeat the same offenses.

Many Catholics have refused to return to the Church or give any support since this has happened. The biggest loss for individuals walking away from the Church is their failure to practice their faith. They have deprived themselves of receiving the Body and Blood of Jesus Christ during Holy Communion. He's the One who gives us life.

We have all lost in this tragedy. The innocent priests will be condemned by the public for years to come. Their responsibilities and blessed honor to serve on the altar have been taken away from them; many were put into early retirement, others left the priesthood on their own, stepping away from the church that they loved. Victims were left feeling anger toward the Church and priests. They struggle with returning to Mass and keeping their belief in God.

Beautiful churches were left with no priests to celebrate Mass. All too many have remained closed. Parishioners had looked at the closings as hassles to travel long distances to a new church. Others just miss the church they attended for years and stopped going completely. The scandal has stopped many from having the will to worship.

We can't blame God for these sinners. Priests are human. They have the free will to choose right from wrong. Those who were tempted into sexual abuse had come under the control of Satan, like any of us. He attacks the weak.

Satan has the power and control over people who have no desire to return to church. He's keeping God's people from receiving graces from the Holy Eucharist and the Holy Spirit, which gives us the strength to handle the everyday hardships. Most importantly, Satan is keeping the faithful from being in a holy state before their time of death. He doesn't want anyone to go to Heaven. The more we pray, the stronger our faith becomes and the closer we get to Jesus.

We shouldn't allow such an evil spirit to take special blessings away from us. Our best protection is uniting again in the House of God. Nothing in this world will make the Church fall. When the chastisements are over, Our Lady has told the visionaries that Satan will no longer reign. She'll triumph over him. If a certain church, or priest, makes someone uncomfortable, they should search for the one that brings them peace.

We are all sinners in this life. If someone falls, pray for them. We have our own sins to ask God to forgive. There's going to be a judgment day and no one will slip by Jesus. Forgive, so He will forgive you.

Eucharistic Ministry

On June 22, 2002, I became a Eucharistic Minister for the St. John Neumann Church in East Freetown. I never truly felt worthy to hold the Body and Blood of Jesus in my hands. Al was already a collector at the 8 a.m. Mass. We never missed going to church unless we were too sick. If I was not able to attend, Al went by himself instead of using me as an excuse to stay home. I don't think Al realizes that his involvement in church activities and services are blessings from opening his heart to allow Jesus to come to him.

As time went on, I started to become uncomfortable at the altar. I didn't feel shy being in front of everyone, but developed a strong inner soul sensation that my serving might not be right holding the Host like priests.

During confession one Saturday, I mentioned these uncertainties. The priest told me that even they don't feel worthy. I was confused, wondering if these vibes were from God telling me this, or if the devil was trying to get me to walk away from this responsibility and lose the closeness to Him. I tried to ignore this uneasiness for a year.

June 28, 2003, Arlene, Al and I were invited by Eddie and Donna Sousa to see their son, Ed, Jr., being ordained as a priest in the Providence Rhode Island Diocese. When a priest is ordained, his hands are consecrated and anointed with the Oil Sacred Chrism and then wiped with a special linen cloth. The hands are anointed by the bishop's hands.

During this consecration, my eyes and heart opened more to my doubts about serving the Eucharist. The four men being ordained had radiant happiness on their faces. They waited at least seven years before finally receiving the honor to serve the Body and Blood of Christ to the parishioners. Their love for Jesus and Mary was unmistakable.

We're all human beings who have sins on our souls, including priests. But we don't have our hands anointed by bishops' hands for this sacred honor. In fact, I was astonished when there was absolutely no education or classes for me to take for such a blessed duty.

It left me saddened not to hear anything about this important task of being a minister. I sat in church with the other parishioners who signed up to become servers. The only training was showing us where to stand on the altar and instructions to fill in if a person was missing on their assigned Mass.

I learned from Father Ed, that Diocesan priests like him make promises, while religious order priests, such as the Franciscans and Dominicans, take vows. They give everything up in their life to serve God. The ceremony was a very emotional experience to witness the ordination. I felt the Holy Spirit during the whole Mass.

Father Ed served his first Mass, and Al, Arlene, and I attended, with pride, to witness the occasion. During Mass, the linen cloth the bishop had used to wipe Father Ed's hands during his ordination was placed around the hands of his mother, Donna. This cloth will then be bound around Donna's hands at her burial.

Father Ed had a spiritual bond with Nancy Latta from Medjugorje after she helped him with his decision to become a priest. The bishop allowed Fr. Ed another linen cloth for Nancy. There had never been such a request. Fr. Ed felt his promises wouldn't have been taken without Nancy's guidance over the past six years. Fr. Ed couldn't be there for Pat and Nancy's wedding anniversary so he made a trip to Medjugorje and presented the cloth to her a week before.

I was in a worse turmoil about being a Eucharist Minister after sharing in Father Ed's special day.

I was so mixed up on what I should do about this decision, until Al said to me, "If you feel this strong about your new belief not serving, then you shouldn't be serving at all."

I didn't sign up again for the ministry in June of 2005. My fellow ministers may not agree with me, but it was my decision to step down. The choice had been painful because I knew every person who served with me on the altar was a good, practicing Catholic. They have a powerful love for the Church and Jesus, as I do. In my heart and soul, I believe this holy honor belongs to the priests.

I had always been taught that serving the Holy Sacrifice of the Mass had to be reserved for males, thereby setting an example and invitation for young men to embrace the priesthood.

I do realize that some priests need help with serving Holy Communion, but there are Masses that have more than ten Eucharistic Ministers on the altar all at once. Another minister had told me that the main reason for this is because serving Holy Communion would take too long to serve the parishioners.

When I had served, I had seen many parishioners, take the holy host and throw the Body of Jesus into their mouth fast, with no expression of devotion. During my ministry, I'd been touched by one woman who openly showed her true adoration for Jesus. When she stood in front of me to receive, she had uncontrolled tears as she took the Host on her tongue. I'd never forgotten that special and holy moment. God had let me witness what receiving His Body and Blood was meant to be.

It had been a blessed and divine honor to have received Jesus this way, and I still do. I only pray we aren't, innocently, abusing His Sacred Body.

I personally miss the old traditions and practices in the Church. There's fear within me when I see the Blessed Sacrament pushed to a side area of the altar. The tabernacle is not a side shrine. In my heart, God belongs always in the *center* of the altar. Isn't He the center of our lives? Is Satan chipping away at our religion hoping for us to fall into his trap?

Father Ed with Patrick and Nancy Latta.

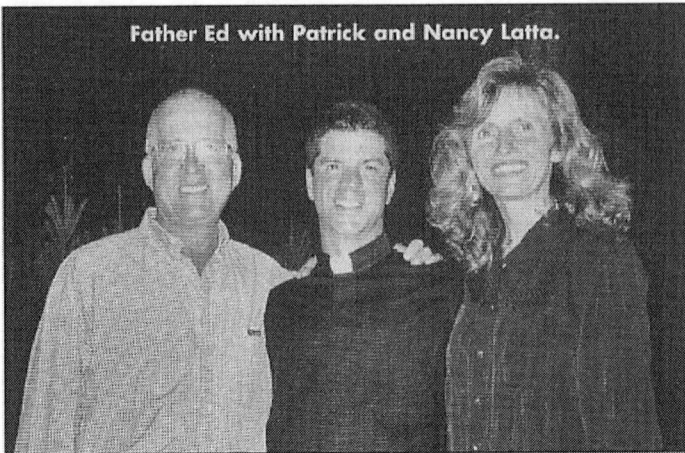

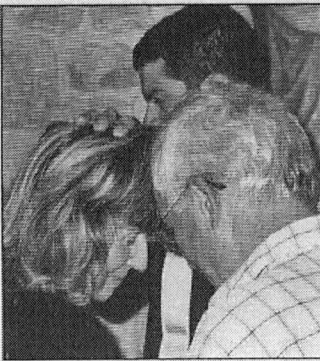

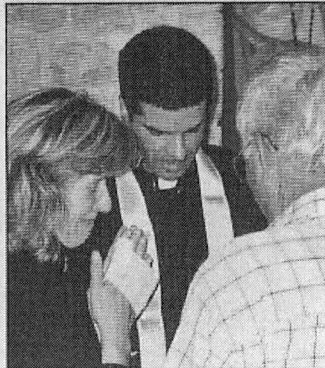

The linen cloth that the bishop had used to wipe
Father Ed's hands during his ordination was presented
to Nancy Latta from Fr. Ed. The cloth will be bound
around her hands at her burial.

The Medjugorje Magazine can be purchased at:
Medjugorje Magazine,
PO Box 37
Westmont, IL 60559.

The Miracle of Corey

On October 17, 2003, my daughter, Lori, called me, in tears, when she and her husband, Mark, rushed to the hospital to see their first grandchild's birth. This was Lori's second marriage and Mark's son's baby. The family was warned by the doctors that the chances of the baby being born alive were very slim: after a sonogram, they had discovered the lungs were undeveloped.

At the time, Lori had been struggling to find her faith. She had told me earlier that she wasn't even sure if she believed in God. This was something I couldn't fathom, after bringing her and Debbie to church every Sunday through their growing years. I had never wondered or questioned if my daughters believed in Jesus. I automatically *assumed* Lori was a strong Catholic at heart, even though she didn't practice her faith. I had strayed myself. I understood her separation from the Church and didn't want to judge her.

I pray the rosary every day for my whole family to turn back to God. I don't believe in pushing them. God gives all of us free will, so I keep my faith that He will call them back in His time. I have always offered my suffering (mentally and physically) up for them. Each day I consecrate their conversion up to the Immaculate Heart of Mary.

Lori was aware that my faith was strong. She begged me to put the baby on my prayer-line and to say a rosary. I explained how important to the baby's health it was for her to do the same. She wanted so much to believe as I did.

To the doctors' amazement, little Corey was born October 18, 2003. Another miracle Dad had talked about: when doctors

215

gave no hope. Corey's lungs were fine, but his kidneys were not functioning normally. In 2005, they were supposed to start testing family members to see if one of them could become a kidney donor. (As of 2011, Corey is doing well with no transplant).

Dedication of the WWII Memorial

In March of 2004, I heard that a memorial was going to be dedicated to the WWII Veterans in Washington, D.C. on Memorial Day. I spoke to my brother, Joe, about the orientation and he went on the website to register our father's name with the rank he had held at the time of WWII.

As time passed, I developed a strong desire to learn more about my father's life during the war. I went on the internet and searched for any information about WWII. I keyed in Col. Albert L. Gramm, and to my complete shock, his name appeared with his unit, the 101st Infantry, 1st Battalion, Company B, of the 26th Yankee Division.

His duties progressively went from: Infantry Platoon Leader, Company Commander, Battalion Operations Officer S-3, Regimental S-3 Division Assistant G-3, the Battalion Commander, and Combined Arms Task Force Commander. He fought in the major battles in the Lorraine Campaign, Metz and in the Battle of the Bulge for which he received the Bronze Medal.

The 26th Yankee Division went into full force after the Germans crashed throughout Europe in May 1940. Throughout the United States the National Guard Divisions were inducted into Federal Service within a year. And so, on January 16, 1941, the 26th Division, the "Yankee Division" of World War II, was inducted and the 10,000 Massachusetts officers and men of the division reported to the 50 armories throughout the state.

Initial training for preliminary field maneuvers was at Camp Edwards, Massachusetts. The Regiment again moved to

Camp Edwards in September 1941. They moved to participate in Carolina Maneuvers during October and November, returning again in December to Camp Edwards.

The world was stunned by the attack on Pearl Harbor on December 7, 1941. For the 26th Division, it meant immediate assignments to the Eastern Defense Command to aid in the security of the U.S.'s East Coast. The Regiment was engaged in shore patrol duty.

Training and preparations were completed in a year, and the Regiment moved to Camp Campbell, Kentucky, to Tennessee maneuvers, to Fort Jackson, South Carolina, and finally to Camp Shanks, New York. On September 7, 1944, the 101st Infantry Regiment docked in Cherbourg, France.

The Battle of the Bulge lasted from December 16, 1944 to January 25, 1945. It was the largest Land Battle the U.S. Army had fought during World War II and to this date. The Ardennes Offensive (called Operation Wacht Am Rhein by the German Military Time), officially named the Battle of the Ardennes by the U.S. Army (and to the general public as the Battle of the Bulge).

The Battle of Ardennes was destined to be one of the fiercest and most trying of all for the 101st Infantry. More than a million men fought in this battle totaling 600,000 Germans, 500,000 Americans and 55,000 British.

After gathering all this information, I placed an ad on the website of the 26th Yankee Division, asking for any feedback from anyone who might have served alongside my father. Within weeks, I received replies back from servicemen by e-mail, personal letters and phone calls. Veterans sent me their memorabilia that they had intended to save for their own families.

Colonel Leonid Kondratiuk, a retired director from the US Army, referred me to the recently published book *The Command is Forward; The 101st Infantry In Lorraine* written by James C. Haahr. In its narrative, my father was mentioned several times (on pages 93, 115, twice, and 140). The book will be a treasured item to me because it mentions many of the locations where Dad had fought.

My father went to Camp Drum in New York for his training. It was a 10,000-acre summer reserve training camp. From 1942-1944, a number of buildings were built for housing and training. During this period, a mobilization hospital was constructed in the old post 2400 area with capacity to house 540 patients. Medical facilities had been erected during World War II. Certain portions of the hospital continued to be occupied to support the reserve training mission.

I continued to search the website for information on Camp Drum, when I came upon a Jim Neville, who was the Curator for Fort Drum Historical Collections. I emailed him and asked if there was any information on my father. He answered right away saying yes, and that he was trying to put a memorial together for the 26th Yankee Division. Jim wanted pictures of Dad and hoped to dedicate a private memorial for him. He

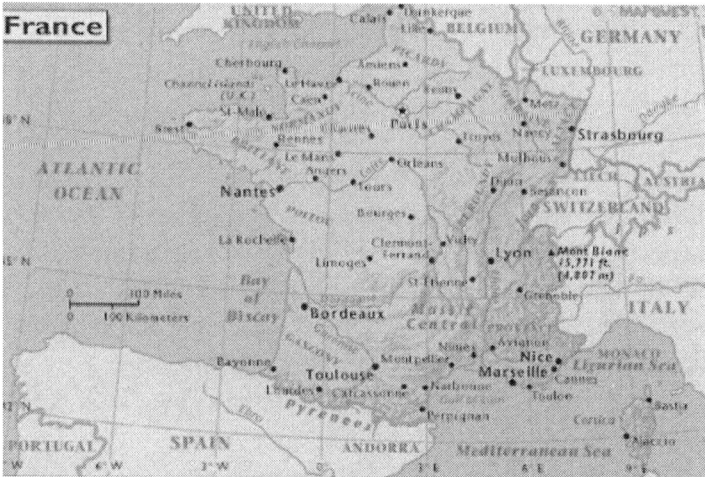

France and Germany Borders (Battle Map)

informed me that very little information was ever gathered about the 26th Yankee Division during WWII so I sent him what my mother had gathered from her scrapbooks.

Jim wrote back to me and through his record searching, he found that a WWII unit history, "26 Infantry Division-Yankee Division," published by Turner Publishing Company, mentions a Major Gramm in conjunction with the German surrender of the St. Jeanne d'Arc fortress outside of Metz, France, on December 13, 1944.

A Joe Devine of North Weymouth called to introduce himself. He and his brother Ed had served under my father. Ed had since passed away. He told me that in 1942, the company was divided into three parts: one third went to the Pacific and one third formed a new unit. He said it had to be a hard decision for my father to decide how to separate the men and split up the division.

Ed and Joe were assigned to the new unit, the 328th Infantry. My father fought to keep the two together for a while, but back then, the military didn't want to keep brothers in the same unit during combat. There had been too many records of brothers dying together at the same location of a battle. Ed had solved the problem by joining a Parachute Unit shortly afterward.

Joe had written his memoirs for his family and was going to throw them away until he heard from me.

He wrote, "You're an excellent salesperson!"

His local newspaper published his memoirs. He stated that the night before the war ended, November 18, 1944, it was bitterly cold and snowed heavily until daybreak. Joe had lost all feelings in his feet and couldn't walk that morning. His medical team diagnosed him with trench foot. He'd been hospitalized in England. Upon healing, his commanding officer asked him if he would return to the front.

Joe told me, "I believe if it had been your father asking, I wouldn't be able to refuse."

Next I heard from a boy named Jared who replied by e-mail that he had just returned from a trip through the battlefields and sites of Luxembourg with his grandfather, Bernard Huntley. Bernard served in the same company as my father, from December to January. Jared had stood on the cemetery hill near Café Schumann where apparently large numbers of the unit had been gunned down. He and his grandfather had walked through the woods to the same foxholes the unit had occupied.

He was sure his grandfather couldn't remember my father because of the short length of time he was with them. Jared stated that the unit was hit particularly hard during the battle at Schumann's Eck and they had merged with another company. His grandfather had also caught trench foot. Jared wrote that Belgium and Luxembourg had not forgotten what our troops had done for their countries.

Bernard Huntley replied back to me on his own and still frequently keeps in touch. He sent me pictures of my father to add to my collection. After Bernard completed his memoir, he sent me a copy so I would have an idea of what the war was like for my father. His stories gave the true reactions and fear the men had had during the war.

Richard I. Paul of Destin, Florida sent me a letter, after seeing my ad in *Yankee Doings* magazine. He wanted to assure me that my father was well remembered by those who survived. He'd been asked to give a speech about the 26th Infantry Yankee Division in combat during WWII, at the Crowne Plaza in Worcester. He confessed there were very few WWII Veteran in attendance.

Richard described my father as, "An outstanding battalion commander." He had had the opportunity to be with Dad in combat and said that he had performed his duties in a superior manner. Richard said Dad was a calm and competent officer. Richard enclosed a copy of his speech with his letter.

Dennis J. O'Brien, of Ft. Myers Beach, Florida, was a member of Company G of the 104th Infantry. He served in the National Guard from 1947 until retiring in 1989. Dennis remembered my father and said he was well liked by all the officers and enlisted men. He sent a picture of my father on the ground, showing the guardsman how to get into the proper position to fire their rifles. My father had worn military khakis instead of his officer's uniform that day.

Dennis said, "That was the kind of officer he was. He set an example for the rest to follow. Your dad was certainly a great asset to the National Guard and to the people who knew him. I'm glad to have known him personally."

Frederick N. Kawa of Whitman, Massachusetts, saw my inquiry in the *Yankee Doings*. He's still affiliated with the Army and served in the Air Force from 1965-1968. He fought in Vietnam in his last year of active duty. Fred had worked with my uncle, Joe St. Onge, Joe Furtado, my brother Albert, and my father at Pyrotector, in Hingham, Mass. Dad's influence helped him get into the Army Officer Candidate program and he was commissioned in 1978. Today he's a retired Lieutenant Colonel.

All the replies that poured in made me realize what personal stories I had missed hearing directly from my father. My nephew, David Gramm, told me that Dad had often talked about the war with him. He probably was comfortable talking with David because he was his grandson. The difference was; David asked. He showed interest in his grandfather's wartime years. Someday, I hope to hear those stories.

Years have passed and many now deceased servicemen could have supplied me with important information about Dad's activities if I had asked and showed interest ten years sooner. Most of Dad's close friends that had served alongside him are gone. They had known him better than anyone else.

Leona believed Dad never would have opened up to me, even if I had asked. She said the only people he talked to about the war were his close Army friends.

I saw the effect of the war when I met a veteran while Al and I were shopping at BJ's Wholesale Club in Dartmouth.

An elderly man, in his late eighties rode by me on his scooter in the store. He stopped and joked with me because he couldn't find his wife, who was somewhere shopping. I laughed and told him he was lucky to have wheels under him to search for her. Both of us talked politely until I noticed he was wearing a Navy cap with a WWII pin clipped onto his headgear.

I asked him, "Where did you fight during the war?"

"I fought in Normandy, and I'm still in therapy because of the nightmares that still come to me."

"You should tell your family about your war years. They'll be a wonderful gift to leave to them."

He told me, "In two hours, two thousand young men were dead on the beach. We had no idea where the enemy was when they were shooting at us. How'd you like to come upon arms and legs all over the place, or pick up a helmet, and see a head still inside it?"

Without any control, the man suddenly went into complete tears and started moving down the aisle in his scooter.

I heard him repeatedly saying, over and over, as he wheeled away from me, "I just can't talk about it anymore!"

I stood there, feeling guilty to have brought up the war. It was so long ago. I was starving for information about the servicemen's experiences to connect to my father. The effect on him made me realize that maybe Leona was right. Dad had probably felt the same way as that veteran—maybe worse, since he had been a commanding officer who watched his men die in front of him. He had to make major decisions for them. No wonder Dad was afraid to go to confession. He had defended his country and lived with the fear that God wouldn't forgive him. Veterans need to believe God's merciful.

The WWII Memorial was dedicated to the veterans in Washington, D.C. on Memorial Day, May 31, 2004. Dad would have been so proud to be a part of the tribute. Who knows, maybe he was there in spirit. I heard that Our Lady allowed one of the visionaries to see and talk to her mother after her death, so anything is possible.

The Gramm family is honored to have our father listed in the WWII Memorial Book along with the other men and women who fought in WWII. Someday, our family members hope to travel to Washington, D.C. and embrace the recognition finally given to the WWII veterans.

Dad on the far left in camp

Military Photo

Dad on the far left with his servicemen

A New Addition

On Sunday, July 31, 2005 Joe and Marge flew to Guatemala to welcome and bring home their adopted daughter, Molly Jeannette Gramm. She was born on March 9, 2005. The family was delighted with our new addition to the family. Dad has to be looking down from Heaven with a big smile and a heart full of love. God brings special children into our lives for reasons even beyond our own comprehension.

Our mother, at ninety years old, was able to witness and hold a new grandchild. What a blessing from God.

Marge, Joe and Molly

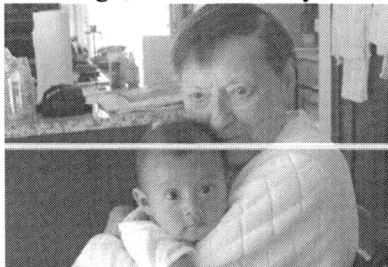

Mom and Molly

Faith Restored

After collecting pictures, written articles, and memorabilia of my father, I started to put his war-life together. Death had waited around the corner and took him when I least expected my loss. It's important to realize that our parents have so much to teach us. They're our history. In the past, they made the same mistakes we're making but, as children, we don't listen or take their advice on how to do things right.

So much time, energy, and sorrow could be saved if we were to pay attention to them. Our own children think we, as parents, are old. They laugh at us, thinking we're outside the times and what do we know? Children insist the world has changed since those *old days!* But morals and worshipping God are fading. It's our responsibility as parents to teach our children about God, prayer, and the unconditional love He has for us.

We're afraid to say the word *God* publicly or simply wish someone a *Merry Christmas.* Our forefathers fought and died making decisions around their belief, faith and worship in God. They gave us what we have today. God *can't*, and *won't,* be erased from this earth. It's His world, not ours.

I believe that from birth, we are placed in a learning process until our death. God puts individuals in our path to lead us to Him. We have to watch and listen for their arrival. Like Dad said, "Take notice."

God wants all of us to share in His eternal happiness. He doesn't judge so much on how many times we have sinned, rather how sorry we are in our hearts for committing them. We were given Ten Commandments to follow as a ticket to Heaven. He speaks to us in many different ways every day to lead us in the right direction, we need to listen; we need to become quiet.

When I sat back and studied my life, I realized how much my father had taught me about believing in God. The most important thing I have learned was to never stop worshiping and praying. He knows life beyond now. He's surrounded by peace and love. I'm sure he knows that material things should not have mattered.

Our days should start and end with Jesus in our thoughts. We're always asking Him for things but should thank him when they are given to us.

In the book *My Imitation of Christ* by Thomas a'Kempis, the author states, "When Jesus is present, all things go well and nothing seems difficult, but when Jesus is absent, everything is hard. When Jesus speaks not within, our comfort is worthless, but when Jesus speaks within, we feel great consolation."

Life never goes smoothly. Believe it or not some of our turmoil comes from us. Maybe we chose the wrong mate, stayed in a dull, boring job, hung out with the wrong friends or had children out of wedlock. If our actions don't feel right...they probably aren't. We can blame God for all our pain or change our choices *fast*. This is where our free will comes into play.

When it comes to parents, try to understand them. Not all relationships are good between them and their children. Maybe you have a good reason for not seeing or talking to them. If they disappointed or hurt you in some way, break down the wall that's between you. If you can't, try to forgive and move on—even if it's without them. Hating and holding anger, can take a lot of energy out of us. Usually two things happen when we can't forgive someone; either they don't even know you're mad at them or they know and don't care. Becoming a bitter person can hold us from enjoying life and our families as God intended. Satan doesn't want any existence of unity within a family. Does it *really* matter who's right or wrong? Pride is a killer. Letting go is a healthy way of healing. Don't let differences divide you. What a gift, if walls could come down, and we started loving again.

"When you stand to pray, forgive anyone against whom you have a grievance, so that your heavenly Father may in turn forgive you your transgressions"(Mark 11:25).

Roles change with the elderly. They become the children, and we're the adult. The dependency can be difficult and depressing for a parent to suddenly need their children's help or decisions are made for them. Aging can be cruel to a once active mind and body. We're all going to get old, if God allows us to live that long.

When my mother was eighty-three years old, she said, "I still feel the same in heart as I did at seventeen; it's my body that wouldn't move to let me do the things I used to do on my own."

Care for your father and mother in their last days. We may be the last ones they see before leaving this world. Let their memories be with a smile and a warm hand, surrounded by family members who loved them.

My father was right about miracles being all around me. I never took the time to look for them or even became aware of them happening. Since he has left this world and time has passed, I've come to see and learn why they went unnoticed.

God hadn't been in my heart and I omitted daily prayer. He would only enter my mind when something bad happened. If I didn't get what I wanted, when it was needed, or my way, I lost faith. I would never freely put my life into His hands and wait for His will. God knocks and we have to open the door.

He needs to become the air we breathe and be part of our everyday life, not just when we need Him. The love from God is beyond our human awareness.

Our Blessed Mother has been sent by Jesus for years to try to get our attention. We can't just sit there and say I believe, and our belief ends there. We have to pray, do penance, and most importantly, go back to church.

Our Lady has stated to all the visionaries that Satan will no longer reign after all the secrets unfold. There will be no more sin. If the world was going to end, I doubt if the visionaries would be having children. God will decide who stays or goes from the decisions we made after hearing all the warnings. The decision factor will be who ignored and denied Jesus, and who has loved and worshipped Him.

Our Lady will be leaving a permanent sign on Apparition Hill once the last visionary receives their tenth secret. They were told the evidence will be seen, but no one will be able to touch the marker and that there'll be no doubt on Earth, even from the unbelievers, that She was with us. Everyone around the world will be aware of this sign. We'll not have much time to convert after the chastisements begin. If you wait, it'll be too late. These aren't my predictions but those which Our Lady tells the visionaries to pass on to us.

The most important act of conversion is turning to daily prayer and going to church. Once we bring Jesus into our lives, we can then see the things happening around us, like the miracles my father described to me.

Pope John Paul II so often stated to the crowd, "Do not be afraid...Never doubt...Never tire."

Prayer is such a simple thing. Jesus will bring the peace you're searching for in your life. It may not be the way you want, but an answer will arrive. Spend time together instead of everyone going their own ways.

I believe during Dad's illness and death, I was reborn with a spiritual renewal in my faith and in coming to terms how God has an unconditional love for all mankind. I have trust in Him that my father is safely home. Suffering is a gift to share with God and our pain should be offered up with love.

The miracle I had prayed for, for my father to stay with me longer, didn't come. God had plans for him. The reasons are far beyond me until we are reunited. Dad was a loving father who put his whole heart around his family. I had choices on how to deal with my loss. I pulled God back into my life, and He's bringing me peace.

Don't stop praying because of the pain. He'll bring you comfort.

"Blessed are those who mourn, for they will be comforted" *(Matthew 5:4).*

Pray to Our Blessed Mother who knows your distress after watching Her only Son die in agony from being tortured. He died still loving each and every one of us, despite all our rejections and sins.

A loved one leaves many memorable things for us with their passing. It may be one small thing, but it's a souvenir to hold onto. I kept a green and white plaid shirt of Dad's, which I wear while cleaning the house. Mom had given me his over-size rocking chair, which I sat in numerous times in his bedroom. What a treasure. The seat holds so many cherished memories. I hold dear a chipped plastic statue of the Pieta which sat on his bed stand while he was dying. My favorite gift is my restored faith in a loving God.

Our Lady called me to Medjugorje and She and Jesus gave my heart the healing I needed. My pilgrimage had been a beautiful journey in mind and soul.

My spiritual experiences are now a blessing. My eyes and ears are more open to the miracles in my daily life since Dad passed away. We all belong to Jesus, and at the end, Our Savior calls us home.

My father left me with precious memories. They're indiscernible to others, but they were many. He was my gift from God. Through prayer, love and faith, I let go knowing Dad's at peace and that someday I'll be with him again.

2011update since my first print on September 16, 2006:

On November 22, 2006, two months after the first publication of *A Healing Heart:* A Spiritual Renewal, my daughter, Lori Cahill, died at thirty-nine years of age at the Charlton Memorial Hospital in Fall River, Massachusetts from her addiction to alcohol abuse.

She was laid to rest at the St. Patrick Cemetery in Somerset, Massachusetts with her father. Her name was added to his tombstone. They are buried two rows in front of a huge, white statue of Our Lady with Her arms stretched out; the one Lori said gave her peace knowing the Blessed Mother watched over her father.

On February 5, 2007, my mother, Sophie Gramm, died at ninety-two years of age at the Cape Cod Hospital in Hyannis, Massachusetts from a stroke. She is at peace buried with my father at Otis Air Base in Bourne, Massachusetts.

About the Author

Photo by Life Touch Portrait Studios

A Spiritual Renewal is a reprint of *A Healing Heart; A Spiritual Renewal* (2006). The version has been revised. The memoir won the "Reviewer's Choice Award Semi-Finalist 2008" by Reader Views of Austin, Texas.

Alberta H. Sequeira was born in Pocasset, Massachusetts. She lives in Rochester, Massachusetts with her husband, Al. She graduated from Dighton High School in Dighton, Massachusetts and belongs to the St. John Neumann Church in East Freetown, Massachusetts.

Her one hour speaking engagements are offered on "My Spiritual Change Within" and "The Effect of Alcoholism on the Whole Family." They are presented to both private and public organizations, businesses, substance abuse recovery programs and Al-Anon.

She is an instructor in a three hour workshop titled "Bring Your Manuscript to Publication." Alberta is also a co-founder of *Authors Without Borders*, and in 2010, she co-authored with the group of five published authors with *Loose Ends*, A Hodgepodge of Short Stories." Ms. Sequiera is also a co-host with the NBTV-95 Cable TV show *Authors Without Borders Presents* out of New Bedford, Massachusetts.

April 5, 2011, Alberta met with Stephen Meunier, Policy Advisor, from Senator John Kerry-MA office to try to modify the Patient Privacy Act for substance abusers.

Contact Alberta at memoirs@albertasequeira.com to request a quote to speak at a public or private event.

Blog: www.albertasequeira.wordpress.com

Website: www.albertasequeira.com

Other Works by Alberta Sequeira

Someone Stop This Merry-Go-Round: An Alcoholic Family in Crisis
ISBN: 9780741454157 (paperback)
Publisher: Infinity Publishing
Price: $18.95
(Kindle Edition) ASIN: B0045JK1Z6
Price: $9.95

Enter behind closed doors of a family's private life of hardships and struggles with alcohol abuse. People living in the same atmosphere will relate to the constant confusion, disappointments, broken promises and fear. Family members become enablers only bringing the abuser, Richard Lopes, deeper into his addiction. This memoir was nominated for the "Editor's Choice Award 2009" and for the "Dan Poynter's e-Book Award 2011." It's a highly recommended read for the abuser, family members, counselors, and anyone wanting to learn what goes on in an alcoholic family.

Please God Not Two: This Killer Called Alcoholism
ISBN: 0741460297 (paperback)
Publisher: Infinity Publishing
Price: $17.95
(Kindle Edition) ASIN: B0047DX0X0
Price: $9.95

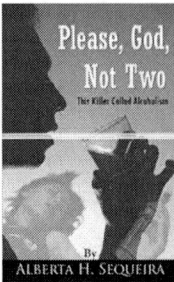

This powerful sequel to *Someone Stop This Merry-Go-Round* is an emotional, touching story of the daughter, Lori Cahill, following the same path as her father. The merciless demon returns making the mother watch the same horrible tragedy unfold for the second time. There are many lessons in this memoir. I guess one could call it a "What Not to Do" book. Nothing is held back from the reality of the devastation that this disease leaves behind.

Loose Ends
ISBN: 0741460718
Publisher: Infinity Publishing
Price: $11.95

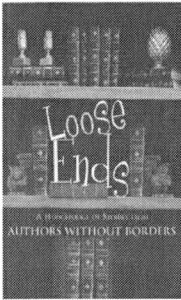

Ms. Sequeira is the co-author of *Loose Ends* which is a diverse collection of intriguing and insightful short stories, poems and book excerpts that will quench your reading thirst and captivate your imagination and emotions. Each of these five published authors approaches their view of the human condition in a unique writing style that will entertain and enlighten any reader. Visit Authors Without Borders at www.awb6.com.

All books can be ordered from
www.amazon.com,
www.barnesandnoble.com
and www.buybooksontheweb.com.